T0165543

Under the
Mayday Tree

Written by

James Grace

Inspired by Love

Printed in the United States of America.

ISBN: 978-1-4669-9104-0 (sc)
ISBN: 978-1-4669-9103-3 (hc)
ISBN: 978-1-4669-9105-7 (e)

Library of Congress Control Number: 2013911623

Trafford rev. 07/17/2013

 www.trafford.com

North America & international
toll-free: 1 888 232 4444 (USA & Canada)
fax: 812 355 4082

CONTENTS

INTRODUCTION

This book has been in the making for 43 years. It has just taken that much time. I spent the first 40 years thinking up reasons why I would even feel like it was something I wanted to do and the next three finding out who that being was who was supposed to do it. Please read this book understanding the intention with which it was written. You will find no footnotes or citations. There are no references for documented facts or hard numbers. Any mention of names implies that I have permission to do so and lack thereof implies the opposite. I don't intend to change anyone's viewpoints or push mine, just to share them and maybe, just maybe, provide some perspective that may shift a few people's paradigms and possibly raise awareness in a world that is screaming for it.

The title came from a place I consider to be sacred ground now—a little spot where I found friendship, love, understanding and always tea. I started to see the world here and realize that I was part of something much greater than I could understand. I came to understand that I and me were in fact beautifully different, and with that understanding would eventually come peace. This spot is in the front yard at Thornleigh Close on a little patch of grass that is lovingly tended to by a man named Luke. It's not the location or the grooming that makes this spot sacred but the time I have shared under the Mayday tree with some of my closest friends and soul mates. I have received messages from the Great Spirit under this tree and experienced aha moments about myself and life. Those things make it sacred to me.

This is a good time to discuss spirituality as opposed to religion, I suppose. You would have already noticed I used the words *Great Spirit* and not *God* or some other word that you may or may not be accustomed to. I challenge you to use whatever designation feels right in your heart, the one that best describes your relationship with that power. I will not judge you for whatever human word you use; I only ask that you open your mind and especially your heart to any and all possibilities and allow yourself to feel the connection.

For me, the journey started many lifetimes ago and will continue for many more, I expect, with my full appreciation of all opportunities provided by the Spirit. Although I am very aware of and happy for past lifetimes, with the exception of a few glimpses, I have not been given the gift of real clarity, and I am OK with that. To that end, this book will focus on my current physical form and how I have gotten where I am today. It will give you plenty of opportunities to judge, ridicule and even call bullshit. Feel free to do so. Just keep in mind that everything in these pages was written from my heart with profound truths and with my integrity. After that, it is all up to you.

STUCK IN A SNOWBANK

My awakened journey started on December 28, 2009, after five or six months of very serious marital problems with my wife of, at that time, 19 years. I was at my wits' end over what was going on. I had spent countless hours reading and thinking about what could possibly be wrong with my wife and how I was going to fix her. I woke up early for work just as I had many mornings before and headed out to the car, which was parked in the back garage. To my amazement, I discovered that it had snowed close to a foot overnight and everything was covered in a thick, fluffy white blanket. I backed out of the garage and headed down the alley. I had to travel for approximately a quarter mile to the end of the alley where I would have to enter the traffic. I knew it was important to keep the momentum of the car up to avoid becoming stuck. Getting stuck in this weather would cause a serious issue for me.

As I approached the end of the alley, I noticed that a grader had pushed a large amount of snow up at the entrance to the road. It was obvious some additional speed would be required to exit the alley. I hit the gas, adding a little extra juice just to ensure that I would not have a stuck situation to deal with. In a heartbeat—and to my total surprise—the car hit the snowbank and stopped, high centred right in the middle of the pile as if that were exactly where it was supposed to be. I stepped out of the car in my leather dress shoes and leather overcoat to survey the situation. Obviously, I would not be driving out of this one alone, and no one seemed to be interested in stopping to help.

Normally, getting stuck and then having people drive by would have driven me off the deep end. Didn't they know I had to work and was going to be late? That morning though, I was calm and accepting of my situation. I started the walk back to my garage to retrieve proper clothing and the tools I would require to rescue my vehicle. After changing into insulated coveralls, winter boots, a toque and gloves, I grabbed two shovels and headed back to the scene of the crime. I rolled the window down a little bit, turned the music up and began to shovel. To my surprise, when I tried to move the car a couple of times after I felt I had moved enough snow, it would not budge. I decided I needed to completely clear the path to the road in order to rescue my Impala and proceeded to do so before trying to move the car again. About an hour later, I placed my shovels in the trunk and climbed into the car to head home to change and drop off the shovels. As I headed down the road toward my driveway, I was quite proud of how I had handled the whole situation—no swearing or yelling and no anger toward the countless drivers and passersby who decided to keep going instead of help. I wondered what that was all about. I hit the gas to clear the snow pile at the base of my driveway. To my astonishment, there I was stuck again and worse now than I had been previously. Already an hour late for work, I decided to step inside to call my boss and let him know I was having a snow morning.

I returned to the driveway and started shoveling again. Now sweaty and tired, I felt a presence and a purpose for my morning. I was being taught a lesson, a lesson in patience and perseverance. It was not clear at the time why this lesson was being offered, but it was clear that it was. As I shoveled well into my second hour, still grateful for the lesson, my neighbor Luke approached. I had not really known Luke before this day, even though he had lived three doors down for the past four years. He walked up and said, "Hey, neighbor, can I help you get out?"

I looked at him and replied, "No, thanks. I think I am supposed to do this myself."

He turned to walk away, and I stopped him. I thanked him for the offer and explained to Luke that I thought he was an extremely nice guy. He looked deep into my eyes and thanked me for that. I was not sure where that came from, but it felt good. I finished shoveling, put the shovels away and had a shower. Once that was done, I called my boss and finished my snow day contemplating what I had just witnessed. That was what I considered to be my first day of consciousness, when I had my first glimpse of awareness and took my first conscious step toward fulfilling my inner purpose. I still had no idea what had happened, but I now had an overwhelming sense of needing to understand it. This was the start of countless hours of conversation and tea shared under the Mayday tree with my now dearest friend Luke. It all started that snowy morning. Numerous lessons were offered to me that morning at exactly that time in exactly that spot, which ones I learned, if any, was completely up to me.

It is clear to me that we are provided with opportunities and lessons exactly at the appropriate time for each of us and in exactly the right amounts for us to process. Having said that, I feel the Great Spirit is always gauging our progress by including a little extra just to see if we pick it up. One message I picked up that morning was patience and perseverance would pay off in the end, but the best message I received that morning—and one I came to realize later—was about being in the moment. By not worrying about anything but the task at hand, I was able to enjoy each second as it was offered by the Spirit and accept each second for what it was. If I had allowed the future in, with such thoughts as *I am going to be late for work, How long will this take? Traffic is going to be brutal by the time I get out,* or the past, with those thoughts, *Last time this happened, I hurt my back; It took hours to get out of something not this bad last time!* my ego would have made sure to wind me up with anger and fear. By staying in the moment, I was able to operate from my core, my soul, and experience those moments as perfectly as I possibly could. I read a great quote that said, "Don't look back in anger or forward in fear; just look around in awareness." This, I believe, is the open door to finding our inner purpose. Think about it. What else does any one of us have except for this second? The past is a memory of seconds already lived, and the future is expectations, hopes and dreams of seconds not yet experienced. The reality is that our past can be good memories and our future bright if and only if we live each second as it is offered as perfectly as we possibly can with grace and graciousness. In order to live these seconds perfectly, we must be in the present, the right now. We must be in love with right now and fight to stay with it. We must ensure we tell only truths and act with the utmost integrity, as well as operate with love for ourselves and all the beings we share this adventure with. When we can love the second we are in, only then will the past and future become beautiful and take care of themselves.

EVERYTHING HAPPENS FOR A REASON

I believe there is no such thing as a coincidence or chance encounter. If something is happening, it is happening because it was supposed to, you have attracted it, or maybe you asked or prayed for it and you just don't remember. Anything is possible, so please don't discount anything. Sometimes, what is happening is as plain as the nose on your face; other times, it as subtle as a word missed in a sentence. There are no ordinary moments; each one is significant and beautiful, and each one is full of opportunity. Through grace and acceptance, we are given opportunities for growth. All we have to do is listen and pay attention; then, as the opportunities are afforded, we at least have the chance to grow from them.

A short time after I spent the day shoveling and learning about everything those minutes offered, my life would change forever. January 1, 2010, is the day I found out my wife of almost 20 years had a boyfriend. She had been with him for approximately five months. The substance of their relationship was explained to me on the phone by the drunken boyfriend. He had recently had a fight with my wife and decided the best thing for him to do to keep her was to try to horrify me with the sordid details. Once I was able to sort out that morning in my head, I explained that I was going to his house to straighten it out. My wife, Marie, agreed that I had to go, so out the door I went to resolve the situation. Luke lived three doors down, and I stopped in to ask if he would come with me to ensure I had backup, someone who might be able to help me not lose control. After explaining the situation to him—please keep in mind that I had only met him three days earlier while shoveling—he replied that we might be going to this guy's house but definitely not until we had had tea together and discussed the situation. We drank a couple of cups of tea and talked. It became very clear that I was not going to this guy's house . . . Luke probably saved my life. What if he hadn't been there? What if I hadn't stopped? What if he hadn't offered to help with the car? It makes no real difference because he was, I did and he had. It was not because of chance or luck but because it was supposed to happen that way, because it was the Spirit's intent for me to begin paying attention. The opportunity was being afforded to me because the Great Spirit loved me and had decided it was time. All it could provide was the opportunity; the rest was up to me, and so began the most intense few months of my life—intense and immensely rewarding. January brought lots of tears and many hours spent trying to figure things out. How could she have done this? How was I going to survive? What had I done to deserve this?

We spent the month of January trying to resolve for each other what had happened and how we were going to deal with it. I told her almost immediately that I had forgiven her and that I would do whatever I had to do to get through this. She explained that she had made a terrible mistake in looking outside our marriage for love, as all the love she would ever need was right there. She vowed she would spend the rest of her life making up for it. We even travelled to Mexico around the end of January to see if we could reconnect and move on. What neither one of us understood at the time was that for the time being, our paths through our individual journeys had separated and as it was intended from the beginning, we had to journey connected in our hearts but separated in our physical forms.

Then, February 11, she left a note under my pillow saying she had gone to get the dry cleaning. She never came back. She was gone from my life. I had no idea where she had gone or whom she was with. I had read every book I could find on what might be wrong with her. I had cried and begged for her to come back so I could be happy again. Nothing was working. What was going to happen to me and the kids? How was I going to go on? What was I supposed to do? She had these answers, and my future was in her hands. How could she do this to me? Hold on—how could she possibly have this much control over me? How could my future and happiness possibly lie with anyone else? Then I realized there was someone else inside me asking questions. Someone else was involved and really vested in how I was going to handle this situation. It was obvious that this someone else truly mattered and the well-being of this other person was of great importance—but who was it?

THE ASLEEP YEARS

At that moment, I could see her gorgeous, 17-year-old figure as I peeked at her through the curtains of my childhood home. This angel was standing on my front porch with her mother talking about attending a hair-dressing school my parents had run for a number of years. I wish I could remember the exact date, but I can't. If only I had realized the significance of that moment, I could have committed it to memory. I stood there awestruck for several moments after she had left with a feeling in my stomach and heart that could not be compared to anything I had ever felt before.

At that time in my life, I had just graduated and my father, through his hard work and an unwritten company policy, had landed me a job in the oil sands that paid an indecent wage and provided anything I thought my heart desired. For a young man who had just been voted by his graduating peers most likely to develop liver problems and one of the most eligible bachelors in his grad year, things were great. My plan had been to attend university and get a degree in biology. I wanted to become a marine biologist and figure out how to help marine animals, specifically the manatee, survive in a world that was becoming less friendly for most of God's creatures. One year, while I was working as a summer student to save money for university, I agreed to a full-time position in the oil sands and quit school.

Just as was intended from the beginning, our paths crossed again when she started to attend my parents' school. Eventually,

I gathered the courage to ask her out. "How about a movie?" I asked her.

She said, "How about a country bar?"

That was it. I was hooked. I knew this was the girl for me! After a very fast three weeks, I proposed by sticking a ring inside a fillet of fish, and with the declaration of our love for one another, the date was set. Unfortunately for both of us, my reasons for proposing—and I suspect her reasons for agreeing—were self-serving. They were caused by many years, lifetimes perhaps, of programming and, in her case and possibly mine, abuse. This is what all of us were supposed to do: get an education, get a job, move out, get married, have kids . . . It was not that easy though. As the months of our engagement went on, we both struggled with our roles, and conflict arose with one another and—in retrospect, I understand—from within. In my case, I was still a child who wanted to party, get drunk and impress everyone with crazy stunts I could only execute while extremely intoxicated. In her case, she was trying to live the life she was never afforded because of her very unfortunate circumstances growing up.

On the long weekend in May 1989, I got a phone call from friends who were partying at a lake lot some six hours away. They wanted to know if I was coming. I ran down the hallway of our trailer right past Marie and asked our roommate Geoff if he wanted to go party in Lloyd. He agreed, and we threw a spare pair of pants and underwear in the trunk and proceeded to remove the roof of my car. I jumped into the driver's seat and slipped the car into gear. It was then I heard her voice. "Jim?" She hesitated. "Can I come too?"

I responded with, "Have you got any cash?" already knowing the answer.

She responded, "No."

I said, "See you Monday," and squealed away, leaving her standing alone on the front porch. This second in time would eventually educate me on how hard it was to forgive ourselves for some things and how important it was to come to terms and seek the forgiveness from ourselves first and then others involved.

Needless to say, when I got home, Marie had moved out and into a spare bedroom at the home of one of her closest friends and her boyfriend. I had convinced myself that it was for the best, as I preferred to party and perform stunts anyhow. Somehow, though, every weekend, I would end up at Marie's. I would sneak into her bedroom for lovemaking and intimacy, each morning telling her it was wrong and should never happen again. She would agree, and I would be off to start another week of the same self-destructive behaviour that had become my life. Then one day, after the couple she had been living with broke up, Marie disappeared from my life. She moved in with a lady named Millie. Millie had become close to Marie through work and cared about her deeply. She recognized how poorly I was treating her and she was treating herself. She allowed Marie to move in but forbad her contact with me. She would eventually screen calls and advise Marie on how she should deal with my egocentric self. Marie became comfortable without me and had even started to consider dating again. It was the space Millie provided that allowed me to see how much Marie meant to me and Marie to see her true value. On an especially dark evening late that summer, I walked into a video rental store to pick up a movie, and as intended, I walked right into Marie's life again. She agreed to a date, and some conversation later, we were back together.

On Friday, July 13, 1990, after a month of marriage counseling offered by the Catholic Church that ended with our priest expressing his belief that our marriage would not last a year, we were married. Marie's family was horrified and mine ecstatic. I was slightly intoxicated while giving my vows and could hardly wait for the party. Marie was wondering why her mom was so angry about the wedding and why she had to shop for a gown alone. She also wondered why there would be no horse-drawn carriage for our Western-themed wedding and why the bridesmaid was not suitably dressed but was also anxious for the party. I found out several years later about most of the issues on that day, and then several years after that, I realized the rest when I started looking inside at my true self. It seems to me now, with the benefit of a little perspective, that all the answers to all the questions were available inside of me and if I had just endeavoured to shut up and listen, I may have been able to hear what I was most definitely being told.

That reminds me of a particular hunting trip I was on in the late eighties where a number of us, six to be exact, were after a moose. With fresh snow that morning, we had tracked the bull into a section of bush about a half mile square—perfectly square actually, as it was surrounded by cut lines. We decided that three people evenly spaced would walk through the bush in the same direction and the other three would take up positions around the section of bush on the cut lines. This should give one of us an opportunity to see the bull. I was to be one of the three walking through the bush, and I took up my position farthest west to begin our northerly walk. Our plan was to leave our snow machines on the south cut line and get rides back to them once we had emerged on the north cut line. It was a very overcast day, making it impossible to see the sun, which normally would have guided us through a walk like this, so I grabbed my compass to get a bearing before we began. I had walked about what I estimated to be a third of the way through thinking I was keeping pretty much on track by walking from tree to tree when I decided I had better check my compass to ensure good direction. My compass indicated that I was off by 90 degrees. *No way,* I thought. *That can't be!* I removed my compass and set it on a tree stump thinking my rifle might be affecting the reading. Nope, I was still off by 90 degrees. Could I really be heading east? Deciding it was not possible for me to be that far off track, I determined the compass was at fault and continued on my chosen path. With my broken compass back in my pack, I continued on my way, eventually emerging on the far-east cut line. I assumed I was on the north line, but where were all the other guys? No worries, all I had to do was head west and then south to the south line to get my snow machine and I would come across the guys. Actually, as I was on the east line, west was north and south was west, meaning that when I reached what I thought was the south line, my snow machine was not there because I was actually on the west line. By the time I found the snow machine and the guys, I had walked almost completely around. I wondered why the guys would move my snow machine. When I arrived, they asked me where I had been for so long and insisted they had not moved my sled. I once again removed my compass from my pack and with renewed bearings, realized it was in fact perfectly functioning. How could I go against my compass, my one and only true guide for that trip through that piece of bush? Boy, I would never do that again.

We immediately started planning a family and timing her cycles for what turned out to be the best sex a couple could have. Unfortunately for me, we were successful almost on the first try with all four attempts, which meant those evenings of trying were over—a sad milestone that I once again missed at the time. After a painful miscarriage, we were blessed with three boys and began our lives as parents in matrimony. As anniversaries went by, our roles were clear—mine was to provide the stuff required by any happy family and hers to provide the stay-at-home mom stuff. Soon, I was working upwards of 1,000 hours of overtime to provide for my family, which ends up being around 100 extra days a year. When you consider on the shift I was working at the time that I was already working 12-hour shifts for half the year, which included an equal number of day and night shifts, this additional 100 days or so was over half of the remaining days each year.

I still had to find time to hunt, party and hang out with the boys. All the while, my bride was left alone to take care of household matters and raise the kids. On November 1, 1996, with three kids in diapers and a wife with vertigo, I departed on a five-week hunting trip. Marie was vomiting every time she tried to move, and our boys were mobile and on a course of destruction. My advice to every parent of boys is to take every material thing you care about and lock it up until they leave home or just take it out back and break it, as that will be the outcome anyway. I would call Marie every couple of days to keep in touch, and each phone call would bring more anger and resentment. She tried very hard to allow me this time and be a good wife and mother, but something inside her was hurting and I knew it. My reasoning in the hunt camp was well intentioned but not well advised; it was all geared around how I deserved this time, as I was a great provider who was working exorbitant hours to provide for them and they should understand that. I chose to finish the trip no matter how hard the phone calls got and deal with the issues when I got home. The moment I arrived home, we sat down to discuss the trip and all the grief over the past five weeks. I immediately agreed never to do that again.

The trips still happened, but they were more broken up with not as many days spent in the field. On one such trip, I found myself camping with my brother-in-law Wes. We parked our trailer in my mother-in-law Marianne's yard and would hunt whitetails with bow and arrow for a few days, and then Marie and Janene would pick us up for a road trip into Saskatchewan. I can still recall Wes looking skyward into a clear blue sky and saying, "It looks like rain." I harassed him without pause for the rest of the day about his farmer ways and how full of malarkey he was. We awoke the next morning to a torrential downpour. Hunting was out of the question, and once again, I was in a position of forgiveness. We couldn't hunt, so we got drunk; by suppertime, we were well on our way and spending some time inside with Marianne and her husband William. I was as always doing my best to aggravate her and show my confidence in the situation. At one point, William leaned out the door to have a look at something, and I decided it would be a good idea to push him out the door and into the mud. I laughed a lot, but I really can't remember if anyone else did. It was about then that we decided to get out of there and head into the Pelican Hotel. We kidnapped Marie's 14-year-old brother Rodney and declared him the designated driver. He took us the 20 miles or so into the bar and hung around while we consumed more than we needed. Right around the time we got caught stealing a crib board out of the bathroom in the hotel, he put us back in my dad's truck and proceeded to drive us home. We convinced Rodney to use my dad's bumper to knock over every road sign on the highway from the hotel back to Marianne's. Wes and I proceeded to load them in the back. At one point, I slipped and fell, hitting my head on the shoulder before sliding into the muddy ditch. I believe that is called Karma. We awoke in the morning with extremely thick heads covered in mud to Marie and Janene banging on the trailer door. Marie was quite excited and urged me to get rid of the signs in the truck as Rick, her other brother, at that time worked for the Department of Transportation. He was responsible for the care and maintenance of all the road signs that currently resided in the back of my dad's truck. Rick still wonders how all of those signs ended up in the gravel pit just a few miles from his home.

I had a great idea. I decided that if I was going to continue hunting, I needed to include Marie, and then together, we could enjoy the beauty of these trips. As our fifth wedding anniversary approached, it was clear to me what the perfect gift was, and I headed to the local sporting goods store to purchase a beautiful 20-gauge over-and-under shotgun for my bride. Surely, I thought, this was the perfect gift and she would see the thoughtfulness included in the box along with a few boxes of shells. I produced the box all properly wrapped in pretty paper and ribbon on July 13, 1995. The box contained the gun in two pieces, and it almost perfectly resembled a box of roses, which I presumed she would figure it was. As soon as I handed her the pretty, beribboned and wrapped box, she looked me in the eyes and said, "If this is a gun, I am going to use it on you."

Uh-oh, what had gone wrong? I had thought this gift thoroughly through. She was going to love it like no other. To this day, when I tell this story in mixed company, I fear for my life. I guess when I can just shut up and listen, I can see whom this gift was really for, but at the time, I was confused and sound asleep.

Working all of the extra hours to provide all of the things for me and my family that we thought we valued, like fancy clothes, cars, trucks, boats, RVs and shotguns, took up a lot of my scheduled spare time and left me tired and feeling a bit lost. It started to seem like I was just a walking wallet and service provider and was missing out on numerous family outings and special moments at home. And yet, when opportunities presented themselves, I would often choose fishing with my friends over something with Marie and the kids. Surely, I owed this to myself, I reasoned. I was providing all of this stuff at my own personal expense. One particular morning, I headed out with Warren for a day of river fishing, leaving Marie at home with the boys. She kissed me and said, "Have a great day. You deserve it; you have worked so hard." With my ego pumped up, we gassed up the boat, hit the liquor store and headed upriver for a day of relaxation. Many walleye and beers later, Warren dropped me off in my driveway somewhat inebriated, and Marie jumped in to go and pick up our car, which I was not able to drive home. When she got to Warren's, she called and said she wanted to stay for a while and have some fish and a couple of drinks with Warren and Mylee. I told her that was a great idea, as she hardly ever got to go out without the kids and I had had enough fun and spirits for the day. I told her I would look after the kids until she got home and to have fun! Shortly after I hung up the phone, I passed out on the couch. A short time later, after not being able to raise me on the phone, she left her fish, her drink and her friends and returned home to find our diapered posse running amuck all over the neighborhood. She woke me, and we argued over who deserved the break more and what the possible outcomes might have been and who was more irresponsible. All this ended with the purchase at some point of something that seemed to make us feel better.

As the years progressed and the kids grew, my resentment about being treated like a walking wallet and missing out grew, and Marie's ability to shelf issues seemed to get better for her. As she shelved and I grew more resentful, the balance began shift, as was predetermined, and we slowly moved away from centre. Our cycle of love and marital bliss into conflict and war with one another grew more frequent. It got to where we would actually talk about how things had been good for a while and we should expect a blowup anytime, as that seemed to be how it was supposed to be. Sure enough, like any self-fulfilling prophecy, we would blow up and go through our war. On the other end, the purchase of something that would make her feel valued and me absolved was followed by a period of marital bliss.

As these cycles progressed and became more frequent, we both felt increasingly unhappy and worked hard to figure out what might be causing this discord. I decided for myself that work had to be the issue—or at least a major contributing factor—and once I had sufficiently convinced myself, I would change jobs, which frequently meant moving our family and eventually turned into a commuting situation. I moved our family seven times in 15 years, trying to fill that empty feeling in my stomach. Why I thought I could fix something inside by looking outside seems a bit of a mystery looking back. At the time, however, the feelings were incredibly real and ominous, and I was doing my best to figure them out.

All of our past life lessons and programming combined with our current life situation programming were steering us toward something, but with our souls' eyes covered by the hands of our unconscious selves, we couldn't see any of it for what it truly was. Something had to happen to remove our hands from our eyes and bring in the light.

MARIANNE

I first met Marianne the fall of 1989 when Marie brought me out to the farm to introduce me to her mom and her boyfriend. Marianne would have been about the same age then as Marie is now, and the resemblance at similar ages is uncanny, especially for a girl who supposedly took after her father's side of the family. I stepped out of the driver's side of whatever vehicle I was driving at the time, and Marie pointed to a double-wide trailer that was in the framing stages. She said, "Go over there and say hi." Marie introduced me to her older brother and stepdad William, although her mom and he were not actually married. Marie would later explain that he was really the best male influence she had ever had in her life. He would go on to explain that when he came into the picture, Marie and her older brother were too old to help. He thought it was too late for them but he might be able to help with the younger two. I said, "Hi," and Marie went inside to see her mom. I climbed the straw-bale steps that were placed against the structure for access and shook their hands. Not many words were spoken as they continued to work and I tried to appear confident and indifferent to whatever might happen. At that point, I leaned on a two-by-four wall stud that unbeknownst to me had not been nailed in place yet. As the board fell away, so did I—right out of the trailer and down the straw steps to the ground below. Hitting the ground hard, I jumped up right away like nothing had happened and looked up into the trailer to see if anyone had noticed. There, Rick and William just stood silently staring with disbelief. It was then that

I decided nothing further could or should be said, and I headed in to meet Marianne. As soon as I entered the kitchen, Marie took my hand and brought me to meet her.

"This is Jim," she said.

Marianne cordially said, "Hi," and continued with whatever she was doing. I spent a few minutes attempting conversation and trying to make Marianne see how nice I was for both my own and Marie's sake. Then, having heard enough, she headed to the back door and exclaimed that she was going to feed the chickens. Marie immediately and excitedly said, "Jim, go with her and be nice!"

I hurriedly put my boots on and headed out the door behind her, leaving Marie in the kitchen. I began asking questions in an attempt to strike up a conversation. "What kind of cow is that? What kind of chickens are those? How many cows do you have?"

Suddenly, she stopped, turned quickly and dropped the bucket of oats she was carrying. "Look," she said, "I don't like you, but apparently my daughter does, so let's just make this as pleasant as possible."

Holy cow! What did she just say? No, she didn't. I followed her around while she finished her chores in silence and vowed from that day forward that the gloves would be off and I would spend every chance I got trying to annoy her. After all, what right did she have to treat me like that?

We would visit often as the kids grew, and true to my word, every opportunity I was afforded, I would attempt to make her life miserable and she mine. This became the routine as we both grew to know and tolerate each other's presence. Then came the announcement that Marianne had inflammatory breast cancer, which, after several months of misdiagnoses, was life threatening. The prognosis never seemed to include a cure, just a number of years she might be able to be treated for. Marie threw herself into her mother's care financially, emotionally and physically. With my encouragement, she became her mother's primary caregiver, earning the nickname "nurse" from all her siblings. I was left to assume the duties on the home front while Marie did everything she could for her mom. Our agreement was whatever it takes, no regrets. We would do whatever we could. Whatever happened, we would be OK as long as Marie did whatever she could for her mom. That way, there would be no regrets if things didn't end well. As the disease progressed and it became evident that it was in fact just a matter of time, the time required for Marie to be with her mom increased. The resentment began to build between us. I was missing her, our family time and my time, and Marie was torn between her family and her mom. We both began to feel unhappy, and we both looked outward for what might be causing the sadness. What we found was each other, as that was all there was when we looked in any direction—any direction but inward, that is.

I was home with the boys the night I got the phone call, and I woke up our oldest to tell him I had to go be with their mom. I drove all night to get to her. I knew how much she loved her mom and how hard this would be. Over the last six or so months, her mom and I had become close, closer than I had ever imagined possible. As she considered her life and the fact that it was ending, I would visit and assure her that I would take care of her oldest girl. She could see how much I loved her, and my love and admiration gave her some peace in knowing her time was limited. It amazes me now to look back and think that somewhere deep inside her soul, she knew that not only was she her mom but her catalyst for awakening and her conduit to realizing her inner purpose and, in turn, my catalyst and my opportunity for the wild ride I was about to embark upon. I can still see the smile on her face that one afternoon in my living room as she breathed from the mask that provided her oxygen during her last few months. I had caught her looking at me. "You really love my girl, don't you?" she asked, and I assured her that I did with all my heart. The smile was all-knowing and peaceful. I still wonder how much she really knew about her part in our lives, how much she was about to do for us and what the outcome might be. That peaceful smile is my fondest memory of her physical form. My thoughts of the time spent trying to annoy her provide one of my toughest lessons about life and one of the hardest things I have had to forgive myself for. The day Marianne passed was the day my wife began to wake up and open the fingers of the hand she had held over the eyes of her soul. As she began to feel the presence inside of her, the conflict and uneasiness became more evident and the need to resolve these feelings became overwhelming.

As this process begins, we are still looking outside ourselves for answers, only now with an awareness of something more inside; it is during this transformation from being asleep and alone to awake with ourselves and our Creator that we begin to see the answers within. For most of us, the opportunity to awaken comes in the form of an apparent hardship or wrongdoing. At this second of my life, I could feel the fingers being pried open over the eyes of my soul, and the first glimpse I got was that peaceful, knowing smile on my beautiful mother-in-law's face.

While we are asleep, we spend our lives programming and being programmed without even realizing it. All of this programming is based on what our minds are telling us. What we can't realize is that this information is all lies, the culmination of each of our life experiences and everything we have been told by everyone around us and eventually ourselves based on bullshit. It is a fact that each of us was born into this world perfect, as intended by our Creator, and the essence of that, the life within each of us, will remain perfect for eternity. It is that perfection, the essence of our true being, that once realized will set us free from the lies and programming that we have been subjected to for lifetimes. It is that perfect being inside the damaged physical mind and ego that is the I inside of me.

ANGELS AMONG US

A short time after Marianne was diagnosed with cancer, we heard that Marie's uncle Len was bringing in a Cree medicine man or shaman to help Marianne on her journey. I had no idea at the time how profound this event would be for my world also. I can still remember the first time I met Clint. He was a man of large stature with a rugged native face and kind, deep-brown eyes. Most noticeable of all though was the immediate feeling one had in his presence. Meeting Clint was a significant event for me. It felt as if I was supposed to meet him. I felt as if I was in the presence of greatness, albeit a humble greatness. He had spent a couple of days with Marianne already before I met him and had done great things for her comfort. Marianne acted as if she had known him for her entire existence, and her only concern was that she would infect Clint with what he was treating her for. Clint explained that she should not worry, as anything he pulled from her, he immediately released to the Creator. It would not affect him. He explained that the Creator would protect him so long as he worked on the Great Spirit's behalf; he was very quick and steadfast in explaining that it was the Great Spirit working through him and his gift was being chosen to serve in this manner. Clint took Marianne's hand and asked her if she believed that the Great Spirit could help her through him; he explained that a lifetime of pain and suffering and the burden of guilt had accumulated to the point where he could not heal her. If only he had met her earlier on her journey, he could have healed the wounds that caused the disease. He explained to all of us in her hospital room that morning that wounds inflicted to our bodies and souls during our lifetimes, if not properly cared for, would fester and cause more serious problems for our physical bodies. These emotional wounds would eventually manifest physically in many forms, and if the symptoms were not treated, they would culminate in serious disease, which, as in Marianne's case, would end our life. He told us not to worry, as everything was as intended by the Creator and that he would work on behalf of the Great Spirit to ease her pain as she prepared to cross over.

Clint looked around the room, and it was obvious that he was peering into our souls. He looked at each of us quietly and then turned to his assistant. I believe it was his brother helping him that day. He was dressed in fawn-coloured buckskin with his hair in a ponytail tied by beads. He was carrying a round drum made of leather stretched over a circle of wood. It had obviously been played many times before. As his brother started to beat out a rhythm, Clint began to sing and pray in Cree. As he held Marianne's hand with one hand, he shook his medicine bag in his free hand. When the time was right, he placed that medicine bag into Marianne's hand and started to sing louder. His brother kept the beat. As I came to understand later, Clint was looking for the pain inside her, and then he went to his spirits to ask them to help to ease her pain. Once he found the source of the pain and the Spirits were located, he asked for the Creator to help him remove the source. With a quick inhalation and sucking sound, he pulled the pain through his medicine bag into him. With a sudden boom followed by an abrupt stop to both the drumming and the singing, he rose quickly and left the hospital room. We all gathered quietly around Marianne to see how she was feeling—each of us with our own feelings about what we had experienced. I was fighting off tears, as I felt as though I had just witnessed something I couldn't possibly understand or explain. Yet, in my soul, I knew the significance.

Clint returned a short time later after releasing to the Great Spirit what he had taken from Marianne, and he told her he loved her. He explained that he had to go pray and rest. He assured us that he was fine and he would visit again and told us all to share our love with each other and Marianne. I caught Clint in the hall and offered him the tobacco Len had previously explained was his payment for his attention. I had bought four packages of pipe tobacco, one for each of Marianne's children and one for the rest of us, and handed it to him. He accepted my offering and smiled. Not saying anything, he looked into my eyes, shook my hand and disappeared down the hallway. I stood outside her room for a few minutes, just soaking up the immenseness of what had just happened. I realized that he had just shared his gift with a roomful of strangers, European strangers, for a couple of packages of tobacco.

The doctors in that palliative care unit still talk about what happened over those few weeks as the disease ravaged Marianne's body. The expectation was that morphine, in ever increasing doses, would keep her comfortable as the pain associated with the disease increased. The reality was that no morphine was administered, and right up to the moment of her death, with her oldest daughter holding her hand, she was pain free and alert. With a soft smile, she looked at Marie and said, "I love you, good-bye."

Immediately following the funeral, we would get to meet Clint again. The same group present that day in the hospital would gather at Uncle Len's farm where Clint had prepared, in the Cree way, a celebration of her life and her return to the Great Spirit. Once again, drumming and singing in Cree, he prayed to the Great Spirit to accept our sister's soul back home to its Creator. Then we all sat in a circle. As Clint prepared the pipe, he told us not to be sad for her, as she was returning to the Great Spirit and her soul was once again at peace. He explained that in all of our journeys, we were heading in the same direction, learning what we needed to learn. He explained that as we walked our lives, we were getting what we needed from the Spirit even if we didn't realize it and that our ability to connect with the source gave us our power to live. He asked us all to give thanks and prayers to the Great Spirit and as we smoked the pipe, to let the smoke carry our prayers to the Spirit. He warned us all that if we didn't resolve the emotional wounds inflicted on us during our time in this world, they would accumulate and cause us physical pain. But we were not to worry about it, as everything happened as the Great Spirit had intended. Two things were obvious to me when the ceremony was over: one, that Marianne was back in the arms of her Creator, and two, that there was something going on here that I had failed to recognize in my life and it was amazing. I knew I had to start paying attention. I once again shook Clint's hand and offered tobacco. He accepted, smiled and went on his way. "Take care of yourselves and each other. I love you and look forward to seeing you again."

It would be the fall of the following year before I would get to see him again. As Marie and I were struggling with what we were going through at the time, we agreed to call Clint and ask if he would see us. With open arms, he agreed, and in separate visits, we travelled individually to meet with him. Marie went first, and then a week later, I journeyed north for my opportunity to sit with him.

I met Clint in a mall parking lot. I climbed into his truck. He shook my hand, and with great joy, he told me how happy he was to see me again. He said he had a few things to do and asked if we could talk while he travelled and took care of some business. I told him I was happy for the opportunity and would accompany him wherever he had to go. Clint explained that his journey had not been incident-free and that his lessons came in many forms also—through addiction and some problems of his own where marriage was concerned. He explained that in that regard, we shared some common ground. We were both average, middle-aged, overweight men married to absolutely beautiful women. With that came some lessons of its own. He used his personal experiences to illustrate for me what was available and being offered by the Great Spirit as I walked my path. He told me that women of great beauty like our wives were noticed by others and that could cause distrust or jealousy, both of which he explained were based in our own fear. In order to serve the Spirit and our life partners, we needed to recognize our fears and not let them rule our lives. We needed to be warriors against the insanity created in our minds, focus on our paths and trust in the Great Spirit. This would allow us to be the people we were intended to be and allow our wives the same. It was when we were able to accomplish this that we would become spiritual warriors and begin to serve the ones in our lives who meant the most to us.

Our first stop was at a house that Clint owned. He had purchased it for his daughter, he explained, and it was being renovated by a man he was treating for addiction who had been on the verge of suicide. Clint had hired him to renovate the basement and was offering construction advice as the general contractor on the job while helping him ease his pain and reconnect. He used the renovation as a metaphor for life. I listened as he explained that each day and each piece of work was where the focus should be and if each individual task was accomplished to the best of his ability with his best effort, the outcome would be a nicely finished basement. Take each job as it comes, complete it as required, and the basement will take care of itself. The worker explained that he had lost a day because of some issues around the ceiling being level and his lack of experience with such matters. After some coaxing, he also confessed that a couple other days had been lost to his addiction. Clint told him mistakes would happen; it was through our patience with ourselves and our perseverance to overcome that we would succeed on this journey. Clint encouraged him to keep up the good work and told him that he loved him. Then, he headed up the stairs. I shook the man's hand and told him how nice it was to meet him and followed Clint out to his truck.

As we drove to our next destination, Clint and I spoke of Marie's visit a little bit. Without going into any detail, he explained to me how we were together but travelling our own paths. He told me how important it was for me to recognize my path as separate and allow her the same. He explained that by becoming a spiritual warrior for myself, I would also be one for her. It would be by becoming her spiritual warrior that I would find what I was looking for in my relationship. He had, in a few sentences, explained my purpose and my journey so perfectly, though I did not fully understand the message at the time. We arrived at his acreage next to drop off some things in his shed. He explained that he would like to introduce me to some of his guests, but they were in the middle of some things and should not be interrupted. He explained that he had a treatment centre for prostitutes with children and addictions to drugs and alcohol. That was his profession. He had attended white man schools to learn the white man ways, and by combining this knowledge with his native ways and his gift as a shaman, he was able to treat many of these women successfully when they became ready to accept the help. He said he just gave them the space they needed to begin to see themselves for what they really were, and once that recognition started, they could begin their journeys to becoming what they were intended to be.

As we pulled away from his property, I told him I had had a dream the previous night. He turned to me with great interest and asked me to share it with him. I explained as best I could recall how I had been part of a band in a smoky bar. All of us were playing our own instruments inside a locked cage suspended from the roof. As we played, I began to hear a voice from the back of the bar singing along. It seemed distant and old and was hard to recognize. As the singing got closer and louder, the bar lightened up. The singer's face became more visible; it was Marianne. She seemed old and frail, but as the singing and my playing got louder, the bar brightened and her face grew younger until she finally appeared young and vibrant with a strong, beautiful voice that seemed to make our playing better. I asked him what he thought it meant. He smiled and said that was for another day, but he felt Marianne and I were doing things for one another. He paused, looked at me and then said, "There is more to you than I recognized. Maybe one day we can sweat and do the smoke together. That made me happy, and we drove back into town where we sat, parked in silence, sort of soaking in the afternoon. Once again, I offered him tobacco, and he accepted, thanking me for our time and offering love and peace. He said, "I will see you again, my brother. Have a safe trip home, and remember our words." I thanked him, and without uttering a sound, I drove the two and half hours home.

I awoke at about 2:00 a.m. with thick smoke causing me breathing problems. My nasal passages burned, and my eyes were difficult to open. They were smarting from the burning sensation. I could taste the thick, heavy smoke and swallowed hard, trying to clear it from my throat. I jumped out of bed and turned on the lights. My boys were asleep in their beds. I had to wake them and protect them from the smoke and whatever was causing it. As I ran from my room into the lights of the house, it was easy to see that there was no smoke. Upon searching the house, I could find no source or problem of any kind. I ran outside to check the neighborhood. By this time, my oldest son had heard the commotion and joined me outside. I asked him, "Do you see smoke? Can you smell it?"

He looked at me with worry and said, "No, Dad. I don't see or smell anything. Are you OK?"

With my eyes, nose and throat still burning, I said, "Yes, Jake. I am fine. Go back to bed."

What was going on? I had to figure it out. I jumped into my car barefoot and in my jammies and raced to Marie's house, thinking maybe her place was on fire. I rang her doorbell, and when she answered, I pushed my way past her and frantically searched for the source of the smoke. With my eyes, nose, and throat still burning, I explained what was going on and apologized for waking her. She said it was OK and thanked me for looking after her. I explained that I had to go and try to figure this out. She asked me to phone her in the morning and let her know how it went. I agreed and headed home. Next, I went to check on Luke and his family. Still burning, I phoned him and asked him to check his house. Nothing. I agreed to call him in the morning also. After convincing myself that I shouldn't phone every person on my contact list to find the origin of my discomfort, I lay back down to attempt sleep. To my surprise, I was able to get back to sleep very quickly, even with all the activity and still very real burning sensations. I awoke several hours later with very vivid recall of many hours of dreaming. I picked up the phone to call the most obvious person I could think of for help.

"Hi, Clint, it's Jim. Have you got a few minutes for me? Something has happened, and I don't know what it's all about."

"Of course, Jim, what's up?"

I told him what had happened with the smoke and then proceeded to explain in as much detail as I could remember the dreams that followed.

I had had three vivid dreams. The first was about a native casino, a very classy, posh and obviously well-run place. As I walked around to get acquainted with the establishment, I noticed some activity at the loading dock. A large shipment of alcohol had been delivered to the rear of the building, and a couple of white guys were stealing it as fast as they could carry it away. I notified the people working in the casino, and they just smiled knowingly as the white men continued to steal their alcohol.

The second dream was of a native ceremony that was being prepared by a native person of extreme significance. I explained that I was not sure who he was, but it was obvious that he was a very significant presence from the native community. As he was ready to begin the ceremony, he looked at me and gestured for me to carry out the ceremony. He would support me. I thanked him but indicated that I was not ready and that I would do my best to support him as we continued. The ceremony was being carried out on behalf of several of my friends, none of whom were native. With my help, this man carried out the ceremony.

The final dream of the night was about me transporting a sacred item from native culture to an address. I was in the back of a truck. We approached the house. Once there, I stepped down from the truck bed carrying the item very carefully. I recognized the house from somewhere and noticed every detail of its construction and upkeep as I climbed the stairs and knocked on the door. The number of the house was very clear, and the feeling of knowing this address was strong. When the front door opened, I could clearly see the layout of the kitchen and living room. It was somewhere I had been before. There, at the back of the kitchen, was Marianne. She was staring directly at me with a very soft smile on her face. As I moved about the house to place the item where it belonged, she kept her attention fixed on me, the smile never changing.

Clint began by saying dream interpretation was something he didn't like to do without an offer of tobacco first or over the phone, but he recognized that that would be difficult and could feel that I needed his help. He said because we were friends and the offering of tobacco had happened between us before, he would help me but asked that we get together later with tobacco to complete the process. I agreed. Very quickly getting to the point, Clint said, "OK, here is what I see. The alcohol being stolen is coming from inside you; it's an indication of your own subconscious and something you must spend some time understanding and healing in order to become a better man." He explained that most dreams were just that and asked if I had had any other dreams that might fit into this category. I offered that

I had been dreaming of Marie and her affair partner often, and it caused some conflict between us. Clint told me these dreams had nothing to do with reality or Marie. It was my stuff to deal with, as was the case with the alcohol. "Look deep inside yourself to heal these wounds," he said. "It will only be once you have reconciled and healed these wounds that these dreams will stop. Listen to the messages to become a better warrior, to become a better man."

Clint continued and said that most dreams were of our subconscious, like the previous two, but there were other types. He called them big dreams. Clint figured the next two and the previous dream in the bar were big dreams. They were messages from the Great Spirit, visions meant to guide me toward something. He figured the native of significance might be him and that maybe we would work together in the future. The other two dreams were a message from the Creator that Marianne and I worked together with a common purpose and that it would become clear when it was supposed to. Clint asked that we complete the process when were able to meet again. He then asked if I would be OK. I thanked him for his help. Before hanging up, I asked, "What about the smoke?"

Clint said, "Find a sweat lodge and sweat with an elder. You need cleansing, and this is how you will get it." He also said that we would sweat together when the time was right and wished me love and peace.

The last time I would see Clint was after a phone call where I explained to him that I had a couple of friends who would love to meet him. He explained that we were supposed to meet and said that I should bring them to meet him the following Friday. I agreed, and we picked a meeting place. I was to call when we were close, and Clint would drive into town to meet with us at a Tim Horton's. I headed over to Luke and Bruce's to explain what had just happened. I told them that I was not sure why I had called; it just felt as though I needed to and that Clint seemed to be expecting it. I explained the plans we had made and felt a little nervous about whether or not they would want to make the three-hour drive to meet him. There was no question, and they thanked me for the opportunity. That Friday, we left early to journey to meet Clint.

As we drove north, many birds greeted us along the highway, and we each commented upon how many ravens and hawks were making themselves present along the way. It was as if they were guiding us on our way. The significance of the birds was so strong with me that I recalled a story from years earlier that I had never shared before. While travelling along a snowy highway in northern Alberta years earlier, I noticed a snowy owl sitting on the shoulder right on the white line. When I went by, the owl never moved. I hit the brakes and turned around. I had been watching ditches my entire life for birds that had been hit and left for dead by vehicles. When I found them, I would get permits and have them mounted and displayed in my house. It seemed they deserved at least that, and they were beautiful to look at. I had always hoped to find a snowy owl but never had. As I approached this snowy owl again, I was amazed that it had not flown away but saw this as my chance to have the bird for my wall. I accelerated and moved onto the shoulder. The bird flew at the last minute, and I heard a thud. I thought I had my snowy owl. I pulled over and went to gather the bird. As I walked the ditch, an ominous feeling filled my being. I can remember thinking I had done something terribly wrong. I felt as if I had hit my spirit guide. Even though I was not clear what that was, I had to fight back a very sick feeling and try not to throw up. I searched for an hour and never found that bird.

I explained to Luke and Bruce that I had never told that story before and that I was not proud of what I had done. I wondered if I could ever be forgiven for it. Luke and Bruce both said they were not there to judge me and that I needed to forgive myself first for the act I was hurting from. They explained that it happened at a time in my life when I was asleep and not conscious of the significance of the circumstance. They also explained that everything happened for a reason and that I should look for the lesson being offered. Bruce turned and explained that my sharing the story and forgiving myself was the first step. The final step was to ask forgiveness of the bird clan, which included all species of birds. He also offered that when I saw an owl again, I would be receiving my absolution from them. It was only a few miles later that a very large grey owl appeared in a tree about a hundred yards from the highway. As we passed, I stared into his eyes and he into mine. As I fought back tears, I remember thinking, *There really are no ordinary moments,* and I thanked the bird clan for my absolution.

Sometime later, as we approached city limits, we all noticed how the birds had changed. It seemed as though the city and all the associated activity had made them confused and less focused. We commented on how it seemed that we as humans were affecting these animals and others. It was then that I started to feel anxious. All of a sudden, I was very concerned about the meeting. I began to question something I had never questioned before: What if Luke and Bruce didn't like Clint? What if they didn't see him as I did? What if I was wrong? What if Clint was not what I thought he was? I picked up my phone and called Clint to let him know we were close. There was no answer, so I left a message. I started to really worry that Clint had forgotten and that our trip might be in vain. I tried him again with the same result. Luke looked at me and asked, "Are you OK?"

I explained my feelings to him and Bruce. I said that I knew it was silly, but the feelings were overwhelming. I didn't want to waste their time, and I wasn't sure how this would turn out. They both told me to relax and said it would turn out exactly as it was intended to; even if all we got was to share the road trip that day, it would be worth it. They urged me to relax and try him again. This time, Clint answered and provided directions to the meeting spot. He said he would be a few minutes but he was on the way.

As Clint approached, he extended his hand to me with his warm smile and said, "Great to see you again, my brother." He held my hand an extra second, and while still smiling, he added, "Don't worry, Jim; I won't let you down." An intense warmth filled my heart, and I realized that I had let my ego sneak in. Everything was fine and would be. I just needed to let myself be and enjoy each second. I introduced Luke and Bruce to Clint, and he offered them books about a tent shake and another healer's experiences as a gift for the opportunity to meet them. We all offered Clint packages of tobacco, and he explained the significance of the offering. He then accepted the tobacco, and we headed for some tea and conversation. Clint looked deeply into each of our eyes and explained my relationship with him. He then proceeded to describe his gift and connection to the Great Spirit. He once again made mention that I was nervous that he might let me down but assured us all that he was what I thought he was. Clint spent the next half an hour describing each of our journeys and many hardships, as though he had known each of us for many years. We spoke very few words as he described with perfect accuracy who we were, who we had become and why we were to meet that day.

By the time our meeting had finished, Clint had done some healing and felt the connection and desire in each of us. He made an offer of a sanctioned sweat lodge in our town that we could use to spread the healing that we all require as travellers on this journey. He invited us all to a tent shake that was to happen a couple of months later and spent a few minutes detailing how special these opportunities were. We must work on behalf of the Great Spirit and understand that all gifts bestowed were its through us; we are nothing more than tools for the Great Spirit so that it might share the magic. It would only be through this type of humble service that any of these gifts would be made available or last for any length of time. As long as we agreed to work on behalf of the Spirit as warriors, the gifts would continue to come and we would be allowed to serve.

A short time later, I received a phone call explaining that Clint had died suddenly and that it was not known why. I hung up the phone and cried for a couple of minutes as I told Marie the very sad news that I would not see him again. I stopped myself and realized the tears were for me and quietly thanked Clint for the ability to see what inside of me needed to be healed so I could become the warrior I needed to be. When I was able to quiet my sadness, I could feel the strength in the spirit world that Clint brought. Everything was just as it was intended to be, and I guess the Spirit felt Clint could help more by crossing over. I will listen to my being, Clint, and strive to be that warrior. I will look for you in my dreams, brother. Peace and love.

Ellen came to me in my darkest hour through a work associate who became a very close friend. I was struggling to figure my life out, and Dayla was there for me every day, as I began to sort through it. When she felt I was ready, she mentioned Ellen's name and offered the business card. That turned into a phone call and a series of events that would change my being forever. After I explained what was happening in my life, she smiled softly and said, "I will be here for you for as long as you need me, but as we begin this journey together, please remember one thing: this is all happening for you, Jim. No matter how tough this gets for you or how deep into a hole you may get, I want you to remember to look up, because standing at the top of the hole will be me and many other friends with our arms extended to help you climb out."

The first meetings would be to discuss me and my journey and to understand how she got where she was. It was incredible to me that a person as light and connected as she was could come from a scientific background. Ellen explained that she had spent 20 years as a crime scene investigator and had learned everything she had come to understand about life through death. Ellen took my hand that first meeting and has not let it go since. It started with forgiveness for self for all past wrongs as they had been identified now. "You didn't know what you didn't know," she said, "and that's OK, Jim. You were doing the best you could." For a while, Marie and I saw Ellen together and apart as we tried to figure things out. It seemed Ellen knew where we were and where we were going but never did she offer opinions or feelings on the process or outcome. She was just there for us to listen and explain feelings and clarify our purpose as we journeyed.

Then came the big meeting. Marie and I were to go see Ellen together for something big. I can't remember why it was to be big, but it obviously was. I spent the days preceding thinking about what might happen there. Marie had moved out and was living very separately from me, but we still seemed to be connected. As far as I was concerned, we were destined to be together once again. I offered to pick Marie up that afternoon, so we could travel together for our appointment. I told her on the way how excited I was to hear what Ellen had to say and find out what was possible. I was so excited that I proposed to Marie on the way and told her how great it could be.

She smiled gently and said, "You are not going to make this any easier, are you?"

The significance of that moment escaped me also, and because I was not listening, I missed the message. After about a half hour of discussion about numerous things, Ellen posed a question to each of us, me first. "Jim, are you willing to work on your relationship with Marie and see where it takes you?"

"Absolutely, I am. I love her and always will. I know we can get through this together, especially with your help, Ellen."

"Marie, same question."

I held my breath in anticipation of getting my life and wife back. She paused for a second and grimaced in pain. "No, I am not ready or willing to work on our relationship right now."

The honesty and bravery from her was impressive, but all I could feel was the crushing feeling in my chest. I cried uncontrollably for a few minutes. Marie took my hand for a second and said, "I am sorry, Jim." She then looked at Ellen and said, "I think I will go now and leave you and Jim."

Ellen said that was a good idea, and Marie walked out of my life. I cried harder than I remember ever crying. All the while, Ellen consoled me and let me feel every feeling I needed to feel. Once again, she told me how great of a man I was and how I was exactly where I was supposed to be. "I know it seems dark right now, Jim, but I will be here for you every step as you find your purpose and your centre. Remember, this is happening for you. If you trust in your path, beautiful things are going to happen for you."

I spent many hours sitting across from Ellen discussing my feelings and why I was having them. We discussed codependency and pressures exerted on spouses and how past life and current life pressures could change us and cause us to act certain ways. Ellen walked me through sessions where I began to see where I was broken and needed healing. Then, in her special way, she helped me heal. As I journeyed with her, she always made a point of telling me how special I was and how everything in my life that was going on was happening for me. She assured me that I was exactly where I was supposed to be. I remember thinking, *Wow, if she is right, I wonder what is in store.*

One particular session, Ellen explained that she and I were going to take a trip together and with the use of breathing techniques and her guidance, we were going to acknowledge what Marie and I had together, release all associated pain, experience the healing and let that Marie go. I went with Ellen to that place, and with her help, I felt everything I needed to feel. In the presence of many of my spirits and angels, I handed my wife quite literally to her passed mother and asked the Great Spirit to love and care for her. I watched as Marie was carried away and then turned and cried for a few minutes. Ellen asked me to feel everything as intensely as I needed to feel it and give it a form. She then asked where it hurt. I explained that it was in my forearms; they ached as if I were carrying a heavy weight I could not put down and was about to drop. "Isn't that interesting?" she commented. "Now what form have you given it?"

"It's a cylinder about eight inches around and three feet long."

"And is all the pain inside it now?" she asked.

"Yes, it's all in there."

Ellen then asked me to think about the most caring, helping and loving individual I could imagine. "Have you got it?" she asked.

"Yes, I see Luke standing in front of me. He is smiling and waiting."

"Jim," Ellen said, "give Luke the cylinder."

"No, I can't," I said. "It's too much. It will hurt him!"

Just then, Luke smiled and very softly said, "It's OK, Jim. I will take it." In that second, in that place Ellen had taken me, with that man standing in front of me as if he were there in that room, I handed him the cylinder. He smiled and slowly disappeared. I came back to Ellen gradually, with a much lighter burden and no pain in my forearms. I had to get back to the Mayday tree and talk to Luke.

When I arrived at Luke's, he was chatting with Bruce and had just arrived home himself from the hospital. I listened intently as Luke explained that he had been driving along perfectly comfortable when all of a sudden, he felt crushing pain in his arms and chest. It was so bad in fact that he had to pull over. It scared him, and he went to the hospital thinking maybe he was having a heart attack. He went on to explain that no indications of any heart issues could be found, and while he was lying in the hospital bed, he had visions of mountain streams and wildlife and a black stretchy material that was holding someone back.

I immediately recognized the scenery and images as almost identical to what I had experienced with Ellen just a couple of hours earlier. I interrupted Luke and Bruce and said, "I am sorry, Luke, but I caused your pain." It was my fault that he had felt the way he had. I went on to explain what had just happened. I looked to Bruce for answers. Bruce assured us that the pain could not hurt Luke although he felt it as very real. It was something that Luke and I had agreed to at some point; we could not just project things like that without a sacred agreement at some point in our pasts. Bruce observed that Luke and I had something very special and although he had no idea what it was or when it started. It was clear that whatever had just happened was profound and caused us all to take some time to reflect on and feel it.

Ellen took me on more journeys as time went on and spent countless hours helping me understand my feelings and my journey. Never once did she offer solutions or judgment, just insight and room to understand. Whenever I call her, it's like she knows I need her and how badly. She will book me immediately if required or the following week, depending on my unspoken need. I went to her when Clint died, and we spoke of many things, including how fortunate I felt to have met and come to know Clint. I also explained that I was sad for not being able to sweat and smoke with Clint and that I had really been looking forward to working with him more. Ellen reminded me that divine timing was perfect and that all was exactly as intended. She paused for a moment and asked, "Jim, have you ever seen a woman shaman?"

Without hesitating, I said no and continued to talk about Clint.

"Interesting," she said, and with the largest hug and most real "I love you," I left.

It was later that evening when I was able to shut up and listen that the answer to that question became clear to me. I explained to Ellen the very next visit that I would like to change my answer to yes, because I had been seeing a woman shaman for quite some time. She smiled and said, "Interesting." I continue to see Ellen to this day and cherish all of our time together. She is an angel on this journey at exactly the precise time and place as intended from the start.

James was born in 1993, the product of a beautiful anniversary lovemaking session. It was the first try, and nine months later, in glorious connected perfection, he was our gift. As with all of our kids, our goal was to raise him to be a happy, productive, respectful member of society. What we couldn't realize at the time was that in our asleep conditions, we were doomed for failure because the lies we were living were being transferred to our boy. At my estimation, it's about the time we reach the age of three that things begin to go wrong for us. Up until then, we don't even know who we are. We are just spending each day directly connected to our Creator and ourselves, experiencing life and the bliss associated with that totally unaffected being—a miniature Zen master not unlike a dog or a flower that doesn't realize that it's a dog or a flower; it just is. Within each second of uninterrupted bliss lies the true secret of life.

Then after our third birthday, the process of education begins, and we start to learn things from all of those around us. We learn the alphabet, and we learn how to be with other kids from a large variety of backgrounds. The first time we are told that if we don't act or learn something a particular way or in a particular time, there will be a consequence, the stillness is broken. We are like a frozen pond in the middle of a northern forest, whose shoreline is molded by the earth around it. Tiny sticks are frozen in time in ice so smooth animals can be seen beneath a perfect picture of perfectly natural perfection. Then, at the shore, a person approaches and throws a large rock into the air towards the centre. With a thunderous boom, a hole opens and cracks form all around it. Water flows above the sunken ice, and a cloud of mud from the bottom blocks the view from above. The person implies that the pond is no longer perfect, and it needs to get back to that former state or it will no longer be a perfect pond. Fortunately, everything else in the universe besides humans is not affected by the lies that come from knowledge provided by our minds through this type of pressure and programming. The pond accepts what has happened almost as if it had asked for it. The pond exists exactly as it is, and without resistance, it continues to be perfectly formed and frozen without self-judgment. It just is.

At around the age of three, people start to show up all around our shorelines and begin throwing rocks. Each rock has its own condition and threat of imperfection; each rock thrown is a reflection of the thrower and his or her own broken ice. The difference between us and everything else in the universe is our minds and our egos buy into the lies. We accept the lies, and they become our realities. We believe the thrower and immediately stop accepting ourselves as perfect. We don't accept anything that happened, and we don't forgive the thrower so we can remain at peace with ourselves. We believe that the thrower is right, we are no longer perfect. We are no longer OK. We resist, fight, kick and punish ourselves because we are not OK. Our pond becomes more broken and muddier, and each time we believe the lies, the damage gets larger and harder to repair. The blame and resentment go to the thrower, and we become victims of our pond, never again to be that perfect picture of a northern dreamscape. Our damage is doomed to grow with each rock until one day, the accumulation of holes causes a dramatic event and something inside of us begins to wake up. We begin to realize that there is more to us and more for us. These lies are just that and are no more than an illusion of the thrower. They have nothing to do with us. The thrower throws the rocks because of his or her programming. The rocks are reflections of damage inside of other people caused by their throwers and their acceptance of those lies. It is up to us to decide whether to believe these lies or not, and eventually, as the awakening process works, we can decide our dreamscape. The rocks can make holes or pass through our ice without causing a hole. It's up to us. Whatever the outcome, we decide for ourselves to love it; we love ourselves so much we allow our dreamscape to be perfect just as it was intended by our Creator. It is this awareness that allows us to see the throwers in ourselves, and with that enlightenment, we are finally able to begin to accept and repair our own ice. With that repair and acceptance come self-love and acceptance. When we see ourselves for what we truly are and truly love ourselves, we are given the space we require to stop throwing. We learn always to look into our own ponds for our answers. Just imagine a world where no one throws.

For James, it started with a lisp. He formed words and made sounds that were so cute it made his mom gush and beam with love. She loved him and these words so much she would write them down and share them with everyone. She would hug him tightly the way only a mother can and tell him how beautiful he was, how perfect. Then the teachers heard it. Uh-oh, he has a speech impediment. "You have a speech impediment, James."

"James needs to work with us to correct this problem or he won't succeed, he won't conform, and consequently, he won't be perfect."

"OK, what do we need to do?"

"Bring James to us every day; we will correct him. We will tell him he is saying these words wrong and he needs to say them properly or he will have trouble in school. You need to do the same. Correct him every time he says a word wrong and inform him of the consequences if he does not learn the right way."

We bought these lies. We ate them just as Adam and Eve ate the apple, and a little bit of damage was done. James started to believe that he was not perfect and he needed to do something to fix himself or he would have trouble. He lost that perfect love of perfection and inside started to wish he could be perfect again. He had stopped unconditionally loving himself just a little bit.

Many more rocks were thrown towards James for the next few years, not unlike the rest of us, and the lies and damage accumulated. Then, around the age of five, he contracted acute disseminated encephalomyelitis, ADEM for short. James's immune system was attacking his brain, and it was killing him. He suffered a week of misdiagnoses that included: it's just the flu, he is being a baby, take him home and give him cough syrup. He was air-ambulanced to the children's hospital where he spent a week undergoing every test imaginable until they figured out what was wrong with him. James had suffered damage to his brain; lesions could be seen on the MRI machine, and although they would heal, they told us there could be lasting effects. James might have issues with learning and living, and he might need help as he grows. "Your son is not perfect," they said, "but with the proper help and enough work, he may be OK."

We all ate the apple that day, and a little bit more of James's love for himself was lost.

It would be a number of years later, after many rocks from parents, family, friends and teachers—all well-intentioned but sound asleep humans—that James would once again find himself in serious trouble. This time, it was meningococcal encephalitis, very fortunately immediately diagnosed because of his history and our intolerance of anything less than extreme diligence. James was admitted to the children's hospital, and within days, he was in intensive care. I will never forget the day the doctor told us to say our good-byes because if James's condition didn't improve over the next 24 hours, he would die. Prayers were flying from all corners of the country; deals were being made between the Creator and certain individuals for exchanges of life including his grandma Marianne. It wasn't his time, and he started to come back to us. It took awhile, but eventually we had our James back. The doctors once again explained that damage had been done and he would have to have more tests to figure out exactly how effected he was by this. James would never be quite the same, they said, but with enough effort and work, he could succeed and be normal. The odds of contracting both of these ailments were staggering; there might be something wrong with him and we would have to keep a close eye on him. Individual progress plans would be developed in school for James because he was broken. Many tolerances to behaviour and ability were formulated to allow him to function in his not-perfect way. James would be reminded everywhere he went that he was not the same James anymore; he was not perfect anymore, but if he tried hard enough, he might be able to succeed. Once again, we all ate the fruit and more damage was done. Now, a big part of James's love for himself had been lost because he believed the lies about his imperfection.

It was a short time after this that Marie and I started our journeys and the marital issues began. All of this came with more rocks and more lies. More damage was accepted and more damage inflicted, until one day, there was awareness for both of us. It was just a flicker at first, and then, as we began to pay attention, there was a little more space followed by a little more clarity. Our ponds had sustained enough damage that we had received our wake-up call; the toughest part of the process was the realization of our involvement as throwers. Forgiving the past, especially in ourselves—although maybe our toughest lesson—was the only way to healing. James is still on his journey and waiting for his wake-up call. He is still accepting damage as his own when others throw their stuff his way, but we now know how perfect he is. We now know how he got where he is, and we have forgiven ourselves for our parts in his damage. This healing and space has allowed us to see him for what he is: perfect. When James throws rocks towards us, we try to let them pass without damage and realize that he throws because of what's inside him. We allow him that. It's not personal; it's not us that he is mad at. He is looking for himself, and we offer guidance and understanding because we were him once and we are a big part of who he is now. He will receive his wake-up call as will we all, and with that comes true love and the ability to stop throwing. When we have all stopped throwing, we will truly all start loving, and then we will experience heaven on earth.

I passed this chapter to Marie the day I wrote it and said, "Please have a look and let me know what you think." She agreed and a short time later shared her thoughts with me.

"It's OK," she said, "a little confusing at first, but as I read, you made it easy to understand where you were coming from. Did you come up with all of this stuff on your own?"

I felt a tug inside. Without responding, I wondered, *Where is that coming from? She obviously wonders if this is my work, but what do I think?* I have read a lot of books, and I guess through reading and rereading and feeling and my experience, a mishmash of my—isms have evolved from some brilliant ideas and thoughts all provided by the Creator as was intended all along. I consider all the authors and angels I have encountered so far to be gifts from the Great Spirit, all placed so perfectly in my path as to allow me the opportunity to awaken and fulfill my inner purpose. I guess I feel it's my keyboard and the experience and the words are my Creator's intention for me. The gift to use in order to express it also belongs to the Great Spirit. Thanks for all that. I think I will just enjoy the ride.

As I left our room, Marie looked at me and said "my pond was so full of rocks there was hardly any room for water anymore." We sat and discussed how we let those rocks hurt us and how that hurt turned into emotional wounds. Those wounds are exactly like physical wounds, it occurred to me, and the only way to heal them is to forgive them and then forgive them some more until they heal and don't hurt anymore. Ignoring the pain, shelving the pain, harboring resentment, or hating forces us to feel the pain every time we are reminded of the rock. This is not unlike picking off a scab before the wound has time to heal. The wound is fresh again, and the process starts all over, extending the healing process and making the eventual scar exponentially worse. If agitated enough, the wound will never heal and eventually become infected, causing all kinds of additional pain and suffering. If we accept the wound for what it is and forgive the wound and what caused it, we can begin to care for it by cleaning it and maybe applying some antiseptic to aid the healing process. Friends or family can help us by talking about the wound and how we forgave the wound and the wound-maker and even our parts in getting the wound. A kiss from Mom and unconditional love from the Great Spirit that we allow for ourselves gives us the space we need to patiently care for all of our wounds until one day, we look down and it's just a small scar that when touched or remembered no longer hurts. It's just a memory—no longer a wound. There is no more pain, and we are free from that wound. Which one is next?

ASLEEP WITH MARIE

Marie's childhood was full of abuse—physical, emotional and, yes, sexual on more than one occasion by more than one man, including her father. These experiences had robbed her of her childhood and any fond memories of family. My childhood, by comparison, was textbook perfect. I was born into a marriage that still exists today to a mother who did everything for me and a father who worked tirelessly to provide for me. Then, just to round off the perfect family picture, I had two sisters, both younger, who would go on to raise families of their own.

Marie first informed me of the abuse at the limited level that she was comfortable with shortly after our first or second engagement—another significant milestone I failed to recognize at the time. The information was like another language. I had no idea what to do or say, and if I remember correctly, I just consoled her and held her, assuring her I would take care of her for the rest of my life. I had no idea what it meant when I said it though. At the time, to me, it meant protect her and maybe even get some retribution for the unthinkable acts she had suffered. To that end, that night, after a few cups of courage, I went to that house on Ells Crescent and confronted Glenn, who was the fire chief at the time. I called him out on the charges. I explained to him how I saw things going down. I woke his whole family and spouted rage and threats for a few minutes. Glenn would not come close or step outside, so I decided it best to leave before the police got involved—not to mention the fact that I was no more inclined to actually fight than he was. I am sure, though, had it come right down to it, I was probably just angry enough to have gotten myself into all kinds of trouble that night.

After that, I decided that I would help Marie get whatever she needed to move on, thinking some outward actions could help her resolve these issues. To my knowledge, four men, including her father, had violated this beautiful woman starting at the age of 12. Andrew, Charles, Dick and Glenn would all have to pay somehow so I could help Marie move on. Glenn ended up divorced; I'm not sure if it was the visit or not, but I am sure it didn't help. It was on to her dad, some cash for counseling, and subsequent charges laid with the crown in Meadow Lake. The court went as expected. I was shadowed by two RCMP the whole affair to ensure I wouldn't get myself into trouble. He lied on the stand and accused his daughter of just trying to get some cash from him. The crown was not able to prove their case, and Andrew and his lying defence walked away without official charges. That didn't go well and actually seemed to add to the pain and suffering. Had I been paying attention, I would have seen another brick go into the wall that was slowly being constructed around her for personal protection.

It turned out Charles, who I think was an uncle, got real drunk one day and fell down some stairs. I believe they call that Karma. I am sure the alcohol was intended to dull some intense pain he was feeling from his life choices. Dick, I have never met, but I always vowed to deal with him when I had the chance—maybe one day.

For the rest of our marriage, this issue was always there. Although I failed to recognize it all the time, it was always part of everything we did. Marie even mentioned that there was a reason that we never had girls; she would never have been comfortable with me or any man alone with her daughter and that was just that.

Marie's older brother Rick was present in Marie's young life and remembered the physical abuse handed out by their father. Hearing about the sexual abuse was tough for him, but it was not a stretch. His alliance was with Marie, and he condemned his father for what he had done, basically cutting off contact with him. For Marie, this was acknowledgement of what had happened and helped her feel a little understood and somewhat consoled. As for her other two siblings, they heard her but continued contact with him as if nothing had happened, and each time there was conflict, another brick went in. We could not visit the family on some special occasions because he was already there, which made Marie feel alone and unheard. Conversation about a recent visit to her dad's left her feeling anger and sadness—more bricks. A couple of times in our marriage, I would talk to her siblings and try to explain how she felt, hoping they would understand and show some solidarity. They seemed to understand, but the visits and conversations continued and the wall got higher.

Finally, it all came to a tipping point when her younger brother's wedding invitation arrived with a note explaining that their dad would also be invited. Well, I lost it. How could he invite the abuser and the abused to the same function? I immediately reacted. "It will be a cold day in hell before Marie and I will be in the same room as him. Damn you for expecting it to happen!" I turned to Marie expecting a smile and a thank-you for protecting her.

Instead, she said, "Jim, I have to go. Mom is sick, and she won't go if I don't. He is not taking anything else away from me. Mom and I both want to see Rodney married, and that is what we are going to do."

I objected and insisted that we would do no such thing. All the while, my sister-in-law assured me that supporting Marie was the right thing to do. She said she was sure I would do the right thing and not make this about me. About me? She had some nerve! I had had two decades of dealing with this stuff and protecting Marie from these dragons. This had nothing to do with me. I would do whatever I had to to make sure she was OK. Well, Marie and her mom went to that wedding, as did I. I spent the evening making sure there was no contact with him. My family and I went out of our way to make sure everyone knew how upset we were with the situation. It seemed like I was doing it for her, and it felt like the right thing to do, but it actually ended up adding more bricks. It was also another life experience that I would have to forgive myself for. It was all adding up.

When I realized that it was not up to me to protect her or actually to do anything for her, I was able to see how one must deal with dragons. I remembered a time under the Mayday tree when I realized that much of my sadness with my current life circumstances was actually fear. It had nothing to do with my marriage but rather with my fear of loss and abandonment and of not being good enough. With that realization, I exclaimed to my closest friends, "Show me how to battle that dragon! I will meet him in the street right now and slay him. Surely, that will release me from his clutches."

Bruce looked at me and said, "Jim, you don't have to fight him; just embrace him and love him. If you bring in the light, he can't rule you in darkness. This journey is only as hard as you make it. You can fight if you want, or you can accept, embrace and love. True healing comes with the light. I have since learned that the bigger the dragon, the more times we are forced to embrace love and bring the light before we truly make a friend out of it. It seems the bigger the dragon, the more internal work we must do and the more intense the healing and emotions are with each pass at acceptance. I believe the Great Spirit guides us into each pass and offers only as much as we can handle at the time. With each pass, it provides more strength for future passes until we are finally left with only a small scar that no longer hurts when we touch it. Each healed wound brings us closer to our Creator and allows us additional space inside ourselves to feel our true selves and move toward our common inner purpose.

I was gifted with a vision one day of the way we exist with the "I inside of me." It showed me a perfect glowing light soul trapped inside a suit of skin covered in festering wounds that had been inflicted over lifetimes. The I inside was not truly able to shine until that suit of skin was recognized for what it was and healed accordingly. Removal of the skin is not the answer, as it is who we are in this lifetime, but the awareness of the space between the two provides the ability to let our true perfect soul shine through while we endeavor to heal and understand that suit of skin. I believe that a yawn is our soul inside the suit pressing hard to get it away for just a second so it can take a deep breath of the universe's energy to sustain it while we are working to realize our purpose. Next time you yawn deeply, pause at the end and become aware of the sensations of energy and your being inside; feel the tingle and intense pleasure a yawn brings, and then understand why yawns are so contagious. Those feelings, whether felt consciously or subconsciously, are all we need. When this energy surrounds us, it affects everyone. Imagine feeling this way all the time. That is our purpose.

SHUT UP AND LISTEN

The words started coming to me mostly through Luke and Shifu; I was spending every spare moment I had with them, trying to understand what had happened and what I was supposed to do. *Take care of you. Be patient and understanding with yourself. Forgive yourself, and love yourself.* What did any of this have to do with what had just happened to me? What was I supposed to do? Every word I had ever spoken was ringing in my ears. How could this be happening to me? *If it is happening to you, it's your fault. No one will ever judge you for what happens to you, only how you deal with it; that is what decides your character.* I surely didn't mean this kind of stuff, did I? I found myself in my garage drinking warm whiskey out of a coffee cup. That was when Luke came to me and asked how long I was going to feel sorry for myself and when I was going to stop hiding the feelings I needed to feel. I agreed to dump all the booze in my house and begin working on being happy. I constantly asked for answers, but the response was always the same: "We can't answer that for you; only you can answer that. All of the answers are inside you. Your salvation lies within. Look inside for the truth." Then came the first realization of why I was acting the way I was. Why couldn't I go on without her? Why did I think I was going to be alone forever? Why was the abandonment issue so strong? Why did I feel like I could never do better than Marie and never really deserved her in the first place? Where was this stuff coming from, and why was it difficult to ask and understand? One of my favourite responses now to these queries is: "Shut up and listen. Just shut up and listen." All we really can do is ask for help and then shut up and listen for the answers. We have to feel the answers and spend our time present and in the moment. We have to notice that there is in fact a spirit inside of us that is perfect and beautiful and serves the Great Spirit and others. We must become aware that our spirit is covered in our physical being and all associated baggage, and that is OK. We must become aware that we need to give ourselves space between our physical being and our spirit so that our spirit can be and we can be with our spirit. At the same time, this space allows us the opportunity to heal our physical being from the wounds of this lifetime and other damages done through life experiences and ego. When we give ourselves this space, we can have true healing and recognition of our inner purpose.

The journey begins slowly with an identification of differences between I and me and some of the feelings associated with the usual conflict between them. This first consciousness allows us the opportunity to start the transformation into awareness. The journey actually started much earlier for all of us; it began on that first day our soul was given a suit of skin and lifetimes upon lifetimes to begin learning and working our way back to the Great Spirit. All of these earlier lessons in our journeys happened in an unconscious state; it is when we notice the difference for the first time that we begin to become conscious of our dilemma. In my case, the first bits of consciousness allowed for the realization that I was in fact a worthy individual who could never be alone because of my connection to the Spirit and all other beings. It gave me the beginning of an awareness that there was more, much more than myself and my trivial issues. That is not to say that my issues became any easier to deal with; it just means I got a bit of perspective. It also meant that I was absolutely not alone in dealing with them. There was something there for me to draw on and trust as I went through this life experience. It was when I saw this connection to the Spirit and others that things started happening for me. People cross paths with you exactly when you need them, circumstances change exactly when they should, lessons become clear precisely when you need them to . . . etc. I feel that during this journey, as is the case with anything in life, some things come easy and others seem extremely difficult—I call these our greatest hurdles. It is OK that some things seem easier than others, and it is OK that we falter sometimes. This is where we need to be as gentle with ourselves as we would be with the most delicate special person in our lives. If you haven't figured it out already, you are the most important person in your life and you need to treat yourself accordingly. Unfortunately, for most of us, we are our worst critics, and to that end, we are very hard on ourselves. I suggest until such a time as you become aware of how truly special you are, you pick someone in your life who is important and delicate to you and treat yourself the way you would treat that person. That will work for now. Once you figure out how special you are, that love will pick up where you left off. As you journey and listen, things will become clearer to you and you will find resolution. You will see things you didn't before. You will understand what happened to make you feel and act certain ways, ways that are not healthy or positive. It is this awareness of things that were hidden to you when you were unconscious that allows the growth and healing that is there for you when you face these dragons. On our journey to fulfilling our inner purpose, there are many dragons. We must face them all, and we must face them many times before they are vanquished. Each dragon is multilayered, and the more layers we remove, the deeper and more difficult the lessons and resolutions. The first layer of awareness of the dragon is what I call an aha moment. In this moment, through consciousness, we become aware that there is a dragon. It seems almost insurmountable in some cases, as we become aware we have to face this dragon, especially when it is one of our largest hurdles. It is through this process that we are given the tools we need to face it and begin the healing process. We start to understand ourselves and get a little more space between I and me. We start to love ourselves just a little more and forgive and be patient with ourselves. Remember, for most of us, our biggest hurdle is something that has been around for a long time. It will not be easy to resolve. It is through peeling away the layers and learning the lessons the hurdles provide that we gain the strength and the tools we need to deal with these issues ultimately at their core, beneath the many layers once and for all. Take solace in the knowledge that these dragons do not have to be beaten or slain but faced and befriended.

The awareness of the difference between I and me is the path. The doorway is the present, and the key is our breath. Becoming aware of our physical self allows our true self the space to be and to shine. Healing our physical self, facing it and loving it ends the conflict and completes the package. When we have completely resolved our inner purpose, we become totally happy in our own skin. As we serve the Great Spirit and others, we can find peace.

If the doorway to our inner purpose is right now, then the key is our breath. Breathing is what provides each of us with life and access to the universe's energy. Breathing happens unconsciously and is a constant until the day we die; breathing at one level provides air to our lungs to sustain life. Breathing in its entirety provides us with our inner purpose, through the acceptance, cultivation and distribution of energy. When we concentrate on breathing, it provides us with immediate presence and a way to get where we need to go whenever we falter. Breath is the key and should not be taken lightly. Breathing techniques have been at the core of many martial arts over the centuries. My shifu (teacher) Bruce is a Shaolin master and has taught me through training and words under the Mayday tree how important it is to understand and use breath as we take this journey. Close your eyes, and inhale for a five count. While you are inhaling, feel the cool air rush over the skin of your nostrils. When you reach five, notice the space between breaths—that split second when you are neither inhaling nor exhaling. Now, exhale for the same five count and feel the now warm air as it rushes in the opposite direction, past that same spot in your nostrils. At end of your exhale, notice that same spot of stillness between the ebb and flow of your breath. Repeat this three times. Did you catch that? You were totally present for those three breaths—nothing else, just breathing. That is exactly how powerful breath is; that is how it becomes the key to finding your inner purpose—to finding *you*. It is only when you are totally present and aware of yourself and free from your ego that you can find your inner purpose and the soul that is you. What time is it? Where are you? These are great questions. If your answer is anything but right now and right here, you are missing that second, and that second is all there is for us. Only when we are able to recognize each second for what it is and truly enjoy it for just that can we begin to feel the peace that goes with it. I listened carefully one day as this feeling was described to Marie. I received clarity through the words about how being totally present felt. "You know how you feel when you are listening to one of those songs that you just love, those songs that make you sing and dance and just feel good about everything? That is how being present feels." Presence provides so many opportunities that they are hard to list. Some are very specific to the individual person. It is the awareness of these opportunities that provides us with the healing and the space and growth that we crave from our soul.

While we journey, the world journeys around us. All of us are exactly where we need to be. All of us experience exactly what we need to experience at the exact time we need to experience it. As was explained to me in a session with a great friend, divine timing is perfect, and everything happens exactly when it is supposed to. Each second is perfect as it is provided to us, and the way we act in the second decides our past and future. It is easy to be perfect in the seconds that seem to be the good ones. It is in those seconds that bring questions, discomfort and pain that we are truly tested for acceptance and grace. They are also where our true self can be found. It is in these times of stress and unhappiness that the opportunities lie, and it is through our gratitude and grace for each second that we can find the answers. I found this awareness when I realized that things were not happening *to me* but *for me*. I received great comfort long before I was able to see the opportunity for what it was or even realize that if I was in fact exactly where I was supposed to be, then so was Marie. Everything I believed to be true for me had to be true for her and everyone else wandering this beautiful planet not only as individuals but collectively. As this awareness grew, it became clear that in order to journey on my path, I had to first accept it for what it was and be grateful for each second provided. I had to act in each second with grace, integrity and absolute truth and trust in the Great Spirit to provide the rest. Fighting to hold onto things or refusing to accept the seconds as they are provided only causes more pain and slows your progress. The Great Spirit has all the patience and love and will wait as long as you need, all the while loving you as you work this out. It will continue to check on your progress and provide opportunities to allow you to receive the healing and growth at your speed. You will proceed on your path at exactly the speed and in the direction you are able to as provided by the Spirit. The journey will be exactly as easy or as difficult as you make it. On one end of the spectrum, you can fight everything that happens, be hard on yourself as you heal and learn and try to force issues and progress. On the other, you can accept the circumstances and love and care for yourself with wide-open eyes and heart to learn the lessons as they are provided. It really is up to you. Surrounding yourself with others who have already become conscious of the journey will help immensely. It allows for open communication without question or criticism and comfort and safety to feel and act accordingly. You will come in contact with unconscious travellers along the way, and through your consciousness, you will be afforded the presence and the patience to deal with them compassionately. Remember, it is only through the conscious awareness that we start to find our inner purpose. No one can be forced or rushed anywhere. We can only offer love and compassion and answer questions when they are asked with appropriate responses based on the layers and dragons to the best of our ability. Everyone is exactly where he or she is supposed to be, and his or her opportunities are exactly where yours are. We must love and care for one another as we journey, regardless of where we are on our paths.

It was some time after Marie had left the house and moved into a place of her own that we found ourselves having long discussions about what was happening and what had happened to bring us where we were on our paths. We compared our progress and wondered who might be further ahead, not aware at the time that no comparisons could or should be made. It seemed as if we could talk about this stuff together because it was going on for both of us at relatively the same time. It also seemed as though we could offer each other guidance, even with all of the drama we had lived for the past couple of decades. It begged the question: should we be helping one another, considering what had happened between us and where we were on our individual paths?

After a long weekend, everyone was a bit more relaxed. We were all feeling summer was finally upon us. Mother Earth, however, soon reminded us of who was in charge and knew best what the planet and all of its beings needed. Fresh snow—about two inches of it—had fallen overnight. The heavy, sticky snow coated everything. As I left my house to head over to Luke's for that morning tea that I had come to love so much, the first thing I noticed was how beautifully the perfect white of fresh snow contrasted with the beautiful colours of spring. It was truly a sight to behold, and I could hardly wait to share it with Luke and his family. When I arrived at Luke's, his doors were locked and there appeared to be no action inside. Although I was surprised that they were not up yet, I was happy that they were enjoying a sleep-in. I turned to head back to my house and let them get up on their own time. That was when I noticed the heavy burden on the Mayday; the sticky, wet, heavy snow was attached to all its branches, and they were weighed down heavily, almost touching the ground all around the tree. I could feel the tree's burden and decided to help it by gently shaking each branch until the snow fell and the branch was able to rebound to near its original position on the tree. I could not get all of the snow off the branches, so the recoil back was only approximately three-quarters of what it would need to be.

By the time I had finished with the Mayday tree, Luke and his family had begun to awaken and unlocked the door to let me in. I proceeded into the kitchen and boiled water to make tea and wait for my friends to join me. I reflected on a conversation Luke and I had had the night before regarding a question I had about who in our journeys we should help and whether there were any boundaries to be established based on a multitude of situations. Luke suggested that I go to bed that night with an open heart and ask the Spirit for guidance and wisdom regarding this matter. I did this and asked the Spirit to meet me in dream. I thanked it for all my life's seconds and everything in them. As I reflected, I could not remember any dreams, big or otherwise, and for a second wondered what this meant. I walked to the window of Luke's house and looked down on the Mayday tree. It looked so much better than it had that morning. I called Luke to the window and told him the Spirit had answered me. He looked down at the tree also and asked what the message was. I explained that the message was that if any of us can lighten the load of another being during our journeys, we should. We smiled at each other in the wisdom, and each of us quietly thanked the Spirit for the opportunity to grow that second. After an hour or so of great conversation and a few giggles, I returned to the window and looked down at the Mayday once more. I called Luke to join me there again, and he did. I explained that there was more to the message and that I had just received it.

"What is it, brother?" he asked.

I looked down at the tree and saw that the hot morning sun had removed the remainder of the snow allowing the branches to return to their glorious heights. If we do our best to love ourselves and each other, the Spirit will take care of the rest. The profound realization we shared through the Mayday tree that day was full of messages and understanding, and it took us both one step closer to fulfilling our inner purpose.

What is our inner purpose? What is the secret of life? What am I supposed to be doing? Do you recognize any of these questions? They arise when we are allowed glimpses of something greater than the individual, something so big it is not comprehensible. As we travel through our physical lives, all of our inner purposes are identical; we wake up and become enlightened. Find out who you are, and understand that you and he or she are not the same. Find that space you need to operate in the now, and figure out exactly who you are and what your connection to the Great Spirit is. OK, settle down. All you have to do is keep an open heart to all possibilities, and you will make it through this book. Remember, I am not selling anything, just telling you about myself. As a young man, I was conflicted in many areas of my life, conflicted without any awareness of the conflict. It caused me much inner turmoil, but without the space, I was not able to look inside for the answers. That is the most beautiful part of this journey we are all taking; each one of us carries our own answers and truths. All we have to do is ask, and we will be answered. As a very young man, I had trouble conforming to authority and what seemed to be an ever-growing number of rules all designed to limit our freedoms collectively so as not to upset some individuals I had never met or even heard of. I feel today even more strongly about this; it seems as a society we are more willing than ever to give up freedoms to politicians and lawmakers through laws, bylaws, whatever. I say live and let live. If we were dealing with one another with love, truth and integrity, there would be no need for laws or lawmakers. As I grew up, the conflicts became larger and more pronounced, and without the space or any awareness of what I was dealing with, I stared drinking to numb the feelings. With the alcohol came more damage to my physical being, which added to what I was already carrying from past lives. As part of a collective conscience, it was accumulating rapidly.

DÉJÀ VU

As I already mentioned, I have not been granted the gift of clarity when it comes to past lives, but suffice to say, I am aware now that there have been other physical experiences for me. You can't believe how big of a stretch this was for me—the Jim from a year ago and the Jim of today probably would not even be able to have a conversation about this and many other topics. But after much conversation, reading and meditation, I am as confident in this now as I am in rainbows—even though I cannot exactly explain why they appear or how they work, I know they are real. We physically experience things that affect us, some of which we perceive as good and others we feel as bad, but it is all as intended. Until properly dealt with, we carry these experiences and their lessons or pain and damage from life to life towards the fulfillment of our inner purpose.

A very close friend of mine, during a particular meditation, witnessed the fiery crash of an aircraft—he had no idea of its origin or type. His vision was in the first person. He looked out the window of the aircraft and witnessed the crash firsthand, and then he saw his spirit flying above the wreckage looking down on the mess. He drew the aircraft and described it. He and another friend were soon able to locate a picture of a spitfire, and that was in fact the aircraft he had seen during meditation. Subsequently, a short time later, in another meditation, he saw a destroyer with the numbers 752 on the side. He ended his meditation and started an Internet search that lasted about 15 minutes. Not only did he find the destroyer, he found information on an operation that included aircraft carriers and aircraft. Upon closer investigation, he discovered the name of a pilot who had been killed during this mission and some details that matched what he had seen in his meditation. Since he was gifted with this vision, he has completely lost his inexplicable fear of flying.

I have had visions in meditation and big dreams that have led me to believe absolutely that I have walked this world in previous lives. Big dreams, as mentioned earlier, are dreams where you are granted visions of clarity and purpose by the Great Spirit. They allow for growth and healing during sleep. They are in sharp contrast to regular dreams, where our subconscious is at work. Through skilled interpretation of these dreams, we can get to the root of our issues. Big dreams are clear and easily recognizable once understood. In one particular vision, I saw war paint, leather clothing, weapons, family and community; it was all there. The vision was of a native and his ways at a time when he was comfortable being himself in his way. This would have been before the arrival of Europeans and the introduction of their ways and culture. I carry tremendous remorse for the way natives have been treated on our continent by my ancestors and my fellow beings, and I believe that combined with who I was and whatever was suffered, that is a formidable foe I will have to face one day to continue my journey towards fulfilling my inner purpose. All these past-life experiences combined with the cultural conscience we all have based on everything that has happened and is happening on our planet and to others create a substantial amount of issues that must be dealt with.

I don't want anyone to get the wrong impression; visions, whether during meditation or in dreams, are gifts from the Creator and are very individual in perception and interpretation. The goal of meditation should always be simply to clear the mind of all its clutter and give you a break just to be without thought. Meditation is a way to practice life; it is a way to get better at being present and enjoying the moment without interruption from the incessant thoughts our mind showers on us daily.

Meditation allows us to take out the trash we create in our minds and to experience the universe in each second. Once we master the art of meditation, it becomes easier to apply in everyday life and frees us from our minds. Any gifts offered while we take out the trash are just that, and it is up to us to pay attention to what is being offered. To be a true gift, it must be acknowledged as such and accepted by the one to whom it is offered.

Consider now that we are born into our next physical form on this earth to continue our journey carrying the pain until we are ready to deal with it. Consider that we pick our situation to be born into to allow us the growth we need to continue our journey. Consider that along with what we brought with us, our current physical situation and current life imprinting are very definitely adding to the baggage we are already carrying. Now consider that we carry this baggage in our brains as part of our physical reality and that our brains are no more a tool for our physical being than our hands or feet. For a short period of time after we are born, we remain connected to the spiritual plane from which we came through the innocence of being newly born back into the physical realm. Once we relinquish that connection to the spirit world, life starts to add baggage based on experience in our current physical being. Keep in mind that everything offered to us through however many lifetimes we have lived is a gift. Gifts allow us growth opportunities at exactly the right time in our lives if we believe divine timing is perfect. All the baggage contained in the brain is constantly held over our souls as sort of an alter ego; this alter ego operates based on all the baggage accumulated, and as we learn to listen to it, it builds an enormous amount of strength and momentum. As long as we are controlled by this alter ego, we will have feelings of conflict and confusion in resolving some issues. These feelings and conflict arise when we dare to listen to our true selves. Although not recognized for what it is immediately, this is the beginning of coming to know our inner purpose, to waking up and becoming aware of who we truly are.

JODY

I believe that people and events are placed in our paths exactly when and where they can help us the most; they are interwoven in the tapestry of our being by our Creator, the Great Spirit. These sacred events and people-angels are provided by us or for us with a very precise reason at a very divine time. It seems to me that as spirits, we decide through divine intervention what each of our life experiences will be, based on what we need to learn and experience to allow us to progress to the next step on our way home to the Great Spirit. While we are planning our next visit to this plane, we also plan the interventions we feel we will need at very specific periods in our lives to allow for the change, which will, in turn, provide the growth of our selves. We make deals with other souls during this planning to come into our lives and help us proceed. In turn, we can provide the interventions other souls require to allow them their growth.

It was a particularly dark day, one when I was deep in the victim's role and trying to figure out how Marie could have done this to me. I had also begun to think that I would be alone for the rest of my existence, as at my age, I probably would never again be so lucky to find someone as I was to find Marie. I realized that I had never felt worthy of her love and that I had always felt less than she was and accordingly, I had better be careful to provide everything and then some if I was to hold on to her. Was I worthy of Marie or any woman for that matter? With everything that had happened, I was seriously worried that I was not worthy or capable.

It was at that moment that I walked over to the computer to pass a little time while waiting for sleep. The kids were in bed, and I was not sleeping more than four or five hours a night with or without the sleeping pills. I had been that way for a couple of weeks at that point and decided it was best to stay up late in order to sleep until the alarm clock went off rather than lay awake waiting for it. The previous night, I had prayed vehemently to the Great Spirit for wisdom and someone who could love me unconditionally in the way I felt I needed to be loved. It seemed I needed that for some reason, and even though I still felt deeply connected to Marie, it had seemed clear she had made up her mind to move on. As I logged on to the Internet, one of those pop-up ads appeared on the screen for a site called match.com. Without thinking, I clicked the link and proceeded to fill out a personal profile. I had never even considered something like this before, and to be honest, I felt it was a pretty pitiful way to try to find love. It didn't seem pitiful that night, and within 10 minutes, there I was, cruising other profiles of people within 25 miles of my postal code.

The second profile I read was Jody's; she was seven years younger and not interested in any kids, but I felt the desire to contact her. I sent her, along with a couple other ladies who were close in location and caught my eye, an email and a wink. It would be the next day before she responded. She made it very clear in the email that my chances of being compatible with her were slim because of what she had read; she agreed to meet anyway because "Who knows? Maybe we can be friends, and you can never have too many friends, right?" We made a plan to meet at a local bar, and I felt confident and was quite happy she had agreed to meet; my expectations were very low. I was just looking forward to some female companionship. She was a little late because of a train crossing, and I waited outside for her. She commented that I was a gentleman and that would be one brownie point for me. I thanked her, and we went inside to find a table.

We had ordered a couple of beers and exchanged a couple of pleasantries when Jody very abruptly explained that it would probably take more brownie points than I could ever earn for her to want to date me. She apologized for the bluntness but explained she had warned me during our phone conversation, and then she laid it out for me. "You are older than my profile said I was interested in; you are very recently separated and still emotionally attached, and you have three kids and a very busy kid life. I can't see this working. You will have to be very special to even have a chance with me."

I smiled and thanked her for her honesty and then very casually explained that I was that special. She smiled back and said, "A confident man, huh? One more brownie point."

We sat and drank our beers, listening to each other's stories intently. She said, "I am so sorry; I arranged to have to pick up my daughter so I would not be stuck here with someone I didn't want to be stuck with. I am regretting that decision now but still must pick her up. Will you wait for me, or would you like to just meet again another day?" I said I would wait and told her to take her time and be safe; I would save her seat.

She returned a short time later, and we drank a couple more beers and talked until last call when the waitress said, "You don't have to go home, but you can't stay here." She told me how enjoyable the evening had been, and I agreed. We talked in the parking lot, did a quick tally on brownie points and agreed to chat again the next day. Good night, it has been . . . something?

Over the next week, we would sit and talk all evening and late into the mornings about everything and sometimes nothing, time seeming to slip away without our noticing it. We talked about how unlikely our match and how many obstacles there were before us but agreed just enjoy to our time one second at a time. My greatest concern was my boys. What should I do? What if they found out? There was really only one option, and it was the truth. I sat them down and asked them how they would feel if I was to see another lady. They thought about it and gave me their blessing, and although I was not ready to inject her into their lives, it felt good to know they supported me that way.

We talked and listened to one another every chance we got for the next couple of weeks, and even though she still had concerns, she decided not to question what we had any longer but rather just to go with it. I was happy and totally convinced that not only had my prayer been answered but that I was a great guy and did not have to worry about being alone or unworthy of another's love and attention. That felt pretty good. It was about this point that one evening Marie showed up at our home and cornered me, explaining that she wanted another chance, that she had made some terrible mistakes and that she would spend the rest of her life making up for them. We cried together, and I explained that I had met someone else, someone who made me happy. She confided that she had heard about Jody through the boys but that was not the whole reason she was there; she had learned a lot about herself through what had happened and felt a deep connection between us. She left that night thinking she was too late and very upset about the thought of what had just happened.

I called Jody the next morning and went to her. I explained what Marie had said and how I felt, and Jody cried and explained that she understood and would have been disappointed if I hadn't considered working it out with Marie for the family's sake after that many years. She explained that she felt our love was right and that she would trust in the universe to formulate our future. "If you love something, set it free, right, Jim?" I sat and held her as long as she needed me to, and she proceeded to explain to me how much I had done for her, how she had forgotten how to love and be loved and how I had given that back to her. She thanked me for our time together and my honesty, and I left her that morning wondering how it was that two lost souls could come together for that short of a period and do so much for one another. A couple of weeks later, she sent me an email and attached a poem from an unknown author thanking me once again, wishing me luck and happiness and expressing, "You were my season." I will never forget Jody for everything we did for each other.

A Reason, a Season, or a Lifetime

People come into your life for a reason, a season, or a lifetime. When you figure out which one it is, you will know what to do for each person. She was my season.

CRAWLING TO WALKING

B y my calculations and through much discussion with much lighter souls, I figure approximately 1 percent of us as collective human beings have become conscious of our journeys towards finding our inner purpose. Of that 1 percent, about 90 percent of us are at the infant stage of our journeys; there is much work to do. As you can imagine, even though there is a huge amount of momentum building towards becoming conscious or awakening, the large numbers means a huge task is at hand. It is our responsibilities as early travellers to tread lightly while helping others understand what we have already been afforded—the opportunities. We must also allow others their own speed and space and provide only what can be comprehended at the time. Too much information can have adverse effects on a person's journey and possibly slow his or her progress. Although it is impossible to stop or reverse the journey, it is possible to stall or slow it through intervention or individual slips. We are on the cusp of the Age of Aquarius and the end of the Mayan calendar, and this means different things to different people. I can sum up my feelings on 2012 this way; the way we have been operating as humans on this planet has provided many technological and medical breakthroughs, and we have been using our earth to provide us with these luxuries. Our earth is suffering from our incessant need for more, and all balance is lost. There are still many left who know the way to balance and understand our connection to Mother Earth, but they are not heard. An entire generation of Aquarian children and babies are with us, preparing to lead us into the light and listen to these indigenous peoples of the earth to return the much-needed balance. It is our job as early travellers to begin opening the doors of acceptance and understanding and increasing the momentum of the shift towards the collective awakening and allow them to help us and our planet to adjust and survive.

Who are these people I speak of, who know the way to balance, and why are we not listening? It's not that we aren't listening; we are just not able to hear yet. We have our fingers in our own ears. Individually and collectively, it is just easier and much less painful in the short term to hide from our truths. It is why I drank every day for 20 years; it is why some people eat, take drugs, self-abuse and on and on. Personal baggage combined with collective baggage equals a heavily burdened suit of skin that cannot on its own deal with the pain. All the while, underneath this heavily burdened ego lies our true selves, our souls, our spirits, just waiting for the opportunity to shine. It is when we see this suit of skin for what it is and start to accept it that way that we can begin to heal it with the awareness of our inner purpose. With the awareness comes the space we need to let our spirits drive our vessels. Once our spirits are in control, we can make true peace with our physical selves. The space is small at first and sometimes will seem to disappear as we slip back into letting our egos drive. This is normal and is part of the process; it is through our awareness of what is happening that we are afforded more space. As we get more space, the feelings associated will fade from our consciousness. We are not to fear as the feelings subside from the acknowledgment of the space and make way for more significant feelings, because our awareness and enlightenment will grow.

In our unconscious lives, our egos always drove and our reactions to circumstances were always out of ego; these reactions were almost automatic and almost always hurtful to someone—mostly ourselves. The space afforded in recognizing our true selves even briefly allows us the opportunity to stop reacting and start acting based on truth, integrity and acceptance of each moment for what it truly is: a gift. Warriors act, not react, and until we can start driving our vessel with our true selves, we cannot become true warriors.

THE ARCTIC—DEH CHO VALLEY

I spent two years working in the Arctic in the Deh Cho Valley between Norman Wells and Inuvik; you will notice I did not call it the Mackenzie Valley—we will get to that soon enough. As I became accustomed to the ways of the valley and its people, I quickly noticed differences at all levels—political, environmental, social, financial, etc. These differences were hard for me to understand at the time, and I found myself judging these people based on my own experiences and opinions (or my ego's opinion). For me, it was difficult because although unconscious, I still had a very strong feeling of conflict and almost betrayal towards these people and the land they lived on. As I spent more time with elders and chiefs and the people who administer their ways and culture, I realized a fundamental and very basic difference in how they were connected to the earth and how much they valued her. They would even tell me, "We don't care about the oil underneath; just please don't harm what lies between us and the oil you seek. The earth is our supermarket and how we are provided with everything we need to live. If you harm that, our people and our way of life will end." That was when I realized it was not their way of life but our way of life, only we had forgotten the connection and the responsibilities we have to our earth. As we built maps of the areas, I took pride in using traditional names almost exclusively where possible to show my interest in and commitment to tradition and their culture.

One evening, when sharing this pride with a white minister, I explained that a specific location on our project maps showed

"Rabbit Skin River" instead of the "Hare Indian River" as Mackenzie had named it and how surprised I was that we as a culture could float past these people so many years ago with the awareness that they were already there when we discovered it and have the audacity to name it anything but what it was already named. He explained that they could call themselves whatever they wanted but that we had named them the Hare Indians and that was what they were. That was my first real look at the collective burden we carried as white people who have impacted these native people's lives in such an adverse way.

This brings me back to the Deh Cho, as earlier mentioned, which was what it was named on my maps. On Canadian maps, you guessed, it is the Mackenzie River. The story of that valley is very similar to that of all landmasses where white people assumed ownership either through bad faith bargaining or force and placed the native people on reserves, had their children sent to residential schools and tried to convert them from their savage ways. They were not listening any better back then either, but it was not time for the collective education or the awakening; now it is. For my part in this, I have asked for forgiveness from the Great Spirit and have forgiven myself for the inhumanities these great people were exposed to. I have dedicated what years are left of this lifetime to making amends and listening with my heart to understand the teachings they offer and apply them to my life and all others I come into contact with. I have also asked for forgiveness collectively for my race and our history and for the wisdom to repair the damage and lay the groundwork that will allow for our history to become proud and our futures bright. I don't see too much difference between what happened to the Jewish people of Germany and the native people of our continent and others, except that no one came to the native people's rescue and freed them from their oppressor and the number of individual lives lost. I think everyone would agree that if lost for either purpose even one is too many.

JAMES GRACE

As I sat in my truck one evening in the community of Tsiigetchic, formally called Arctic Red River by the white man, I watched one of the village's elders leave his house. It was about 50 below that evening, and I noticed how clear the sky was and how cold the wind blowing up the Deh Cho must have been at that temperature. He pulled a small sleigh behind him as he walked the mile or so down to the river, and I wondered what he was up to that very cold evening. His gait was casual but purposeful. He was very calm and resolved to whatever task was at hand. When he arrived at the river a short time later, I watched as he pulled an axe out of his sleigh and began to chip away at the ice to reestablish a hole that he was obviously tending to. Once the hole was opened again, he began to pull his net out from under the ice. As he pulled the net, he mindfully watched for fish. After about 20 feet of net, there it was: a 20-pound fish. He carefully removed it from the net and placed the fish in the sleigh. He spent about 20 minutes replacing the net and the axe and then grabbed the rope handle on the sleigh and headed back up the hill to Tsiigetchic. He was there for supper. That evening, he was having fish, and he was happy to be provided it by the Great Spirit. As he walked the mile or so up the hill to his home, I thought about my home. How many people did I know who would even consider this as acceptable? How many people did I know who would even have an idea of where the fish they bought at the grocery store came from or how it was handled?

How many people did I know who could even survive these conditions?

Most people live without furnaces or even gas, and electricity is not available to everyone. On one particular evening, an elder asked me what would happen to my people in Calgary if the temperature dropped to minus 50 and the power and gas were cut off even for one night. I explained that there would likely be many dead by morning. How could this be possible? How did we get so far off track? How could we accept something for our native brothers that we could not even survive? How could we let ourselves get so far away from Mother Earth to even allow it to become an option? These people I speak of are the native peoples of our lands and others; they still have a tremendous awareness of the connection between human beings and the planet we share. Even though they have been treated the way they have been, they continue to spread that message and do those teachings. Even some of their own people are beginning to turn the way of the white man and chase dollars with no regard for the earth because of the incessant pressure put on them by us and others to conform and change with the times. Thank God they still are there for us. Now it is time to wake up and look for the truths that can save our kind. We must look to the ones who know the way and respect and understand the balance.

After working in the Arctic for those two winters and a subsequent couple of years to sort out what had happened, I sent the following letter of thanks. I thought I would share it with you.

When I first got the news that I would be managing a project in the Deh Cho Valley north of the Arctic Circle, I was excited and eager to prove my worth to my employer and to win over the northern residents and show them how beneficial this project would be to them and by default to me. I was drawn to the north and intrigued by the people who live there but at the same time was there to do a job and had to find a way to execute a schedule that was aggressive to say the least.

Land access and benefits agreements, meetings with all the communities and their elders, INAC and the land and water use boards, transboundary negotiations, logistics that don't even make sense to anyone who has not worked in the valley, flights and weather, federal legislation, etc.—it seemed that these people just made it tough to work in the Arctic. Don't they understand how good this will be for them? I figured these northern residents to be years behind industry and their priorities not defined; it was up to me to make them understand how important and beneficial this really was to them.

I look back now and realize the understanding required was by me and all others in industry and by our collective consciousness. These people have been dealing with intrusion by white men for many years and from the very first time Mackenzie floated down the valley by men who did not understand the cultures or the connection to the land and of the land to all things. We have been pushing our ways on these people in religion, education, politics, industry and environment for many years with no collective understanding of how that has affected them.

I have come to realize that the awareness required was granted but not to whom I thought required it. I see that awareness now as a gift from the Great Spirit and that gift was bestowed on me through all of the people of the land in that beautiful valley. It is not the elders or the chiefs or the people living off the land who need to understand, change, or try to get it. It is the rest of us, the ones who caused the grief and suffering to our native brothers and sisters over the past many years and continue to chase dollars and inflict pain and suffering through our insatiable need for more.

There needs to be balance on this planet; balance is the only thing that will save our kind. Instead of taking all the time and continually hurting Mother Earth, we all need to slow down and listen to those who know, those who are closest to her. Talk to the elders and the ones living off the land and really listen. Don't listen with greedy ears; listen with open hearts. I now have begun to hear the words spoken to me by these people, and only now do I understand what the message is.

In an area where a small number of people living in conditions that the rest of Canada could not understand and would not tolerate, there is a vast understanding and connection with everything on this earth and in the universe around them. And yet we dare to expect that these cultures change to allow for our needs to be met and would allow massive ingress of men and machinery required to achieve these means to an end. Slow down, people. Slow down and smell the roses. Listen to these women and men. Learn the lessons that are available to us before it's too late, if it isn't already.

For my awareness and understanding, I say to these people, Mahsi, and to all who have the privilege and honor of meeting them or working with them in the present or in the future, I pray for integrity, truth and the wisdom to help them understand and feel who is actually doing it right. Maybe if we all make amends for past wrongs and forgive ourselves, the collective pain and hurt could be diminished to a level where we could really start to listen and learn from the people who know best how to attain the balance that is required for our kind to survive.

SOUL-SEARCHING

When I realized that all of the things in my life were happening for me and not to me and I was able to accept my seconds for what they were, be grateful for them and act in them as a warrior would, I was given a great deal of space. This space allowed me to look around me and understand that my situation was not unique or even particularly bad in comparison. It was roughly this time that Erin offered me her Bible and suggested I read the story of Job. Once again, an angel had stepped into my path and offered me exactly what I needed exactly when I needed it. There are no accidents, and everything happens for a reason. I read the book of Job and realized the lesson: the importance of every second and the importance of accepting whatever it is as it is and being thankful for it, because that is the only way to live a second. It was after reading Job that I started to see more of the picture. I started to see that Marie was on a journey of her own, and she too was exactly where she needed to be exactly when she needed to be there. There was a reason for her in all of this as there was for me, and I had to accept all of these seconds and be thankful for them and the opportunities they offered.

The soul-searching that followed from my new state of awareness was and is mind boggling—Who am I? Who was I? What was my part in this? How do I resolve it? How do I forgive myself and Marie and move on with each second? I found deep-seated issues around abandonment, self-esteem, loss, being alone, not being good enough and many other areas I didn't even know existed. I was able to see 20 years of screwed-up priorities and misguided intentions on my part and start to forgive the I inside of me. As I began to recognize these differences and started the healing process, I was able to begin to truly see Marie for what is at her centre, and although I had seen plenty of glimpses of her over the years, I had never recognized her for what she was. I can see now that there was a divine intervention and it was done for both our sakes. It started us on our own paths of awakening and realizing our inner purposes.

For us now, our paths have separated, leaving our physical selves apart as we work to realize who we are and what are true paths are. We both feel our spirits are still connected and have been for many years and possibly lifetimes but agree to try to live each second as best we can and let the rest take care of itself. I am not going to lie to you; with our new levels of awareness, we can both see where our egos were going wrong and both have commented on how much better the past 20 years could have been had we known what we didn't know. We both have also commented on how great it would be if once we had progressed enough on our individual journeys, our paths could cross again and allow us the opportunity to be together with this new level of consciousness. We are very aware of how fulfilling this could be and also very aware that the only way for our futures to be bright is to live perfectly in each second and let the Great Spirit decide the rest.

IT'S CROWDED IN HERE

In any relationship, there are four people—the I inside me multiplied by two. When we are unconscious, the ego steers the vessel and our true self sits in the background looking for opportunities to inject itself into our lives. The whole time our ego is in control, we suffer from the conflicts and unrealized inner turmoil, building our collective baggage and, yes, even adding to our partner's. Our egos have become strong at this point and have no interest in relinquishing any power to anyone. As individuals, we have built walls by collecting this baggage and have in many cases begun to blame our partners for our own grief. At some point, either through an awakening process or just through a clash of the egos, a change occurs when something causes us to reevaluate our condition. When this conflict arises and the awakening process has not begun yet for either party or both are still unconscious, it becomes a battle of egos. In this situation, no one wins, and it can quickly degenerate into your stereotypical bitter separation and divorce, where there absolutely needs to be a winner and a loser. Someone has to be right, and someone has to be wrong. Someone is at fault for something, and someone is a victim of something. In this situation, even the most innocent of conversation or interaction can become explosive and a source of argument as each individual ego begins to feed on the other. When we realize that there never has to be a winner or a loser and that in our relationships and life, we are all equal to each other and the Great Spirit, we can begin to live. In this life, we are all part of a living, breathing tapestry in which we are all connected to each other either directly or indirectly through an enormous and intricate web of fibres created and provided by the Great Spirit. Each individual soul is directly connected to the source, our Creator, the Great Spirit.

When we first venture out into whichever plane we are starting our journey on, our individual connection to the Great Spirit is through a long fibre extending us through a vast number of other fibres and souls to the outer reaches of the tapestry. In order to achieve our inner purpose, we must experience our lives and learn our lessons on behalf of the Great Spirit. We must then begin the process of awakening. As we take these steps, our individual fibres are shortened and the Great Spirit watches our progress. It winds us a little closer, each wind bringing us to a new spot in the tapestry. Every spot has new fibres in which there are new connections, the realization of existing ones and sacred lessons. These places also provide new souls. Some are just acquaintances whom we get to know for fleeting moments at that specific length of fibre; others, we soon realize, are interwoven with us in the tapestry, and others were placed by angels in the tapestry at exactly the right time to help us find our way. None of these fibres or souls are there by chance. All are predetermined and specifically arranged to provide us with the wisdom, strength and help exactly when required to continue and eventually complete our journeys. We have free will, and it is granted by the Spirit, who allows us the latitude to make individual choices as we work our way through the tapestry.

When we begin our journeys and are operating unconsciously, we make individual choices that may take us off our direct paths and move us laterally through the tapestry sometimes a great distance to avoid pain or conflict. It is when we make these types of decisions that we encounter resistance in our journeys. Imagine our direct fibres being interwoven and even entangled around other fibres and souls as we work to get away from our chosen paths. All these encounters are provided by the Spirit, and all eventually provide the information we require, but as the Great Spirit winds us in, we must be pulled back through this entanglement we worked ourselves into. It is like a garden hose being reeled back in after it has been wrapped around every tree in your yard. Imagine if we had the wisdom and the knowledge that all we have to do is be and experience every fibre and soul as it is laid out for us while the Great Spirit winds us back to it. Think how comfortable that can be if we accept our path and everything we encounter as exactly what it is supposed to be. Don't fret over this; we all move laterally as we attempt to operate unconsciously and serve our physical beings and egos. Through the encounters and our evolving consciousness, we begin to take inventory and awaken to our journey. It is this awareness that allows us the space we need to trust and be that soul connected individually to our Creator. We must allow ourselves to be gently wound back towards that centre through whatever part of the fabric we are supposed to experience. As we are pulled back, sometimes, we will encounter snags. When we are aware, we will allow ourselves to see these snags for exactly what they are: opportunities for growth and healing, not something that is our fault and not something to be upset about. It is all just part of the process. We will gain great comfort in knowing it's OK to be snagged from time to time; this is exactly where we are supposed to be on our trip through the fabric back to our Creator, and the knowledge that the winding will not force us through any snags just provides the tension required to allow us our movement at exactly the time it is required until we have cleared the snag. There is never any extra pressure or judgment from the one winding, only love, compassion and never-ending patience as we find our way through. It truly is when we relax and just be as the Great Spirit winds us towards home that we can find our inner purpose and experience the journey for exactly what it is.

GROWING PAINS (THE POISONOUS DART)

If I believe that I am exactly where I am supposed to be, that nothing happens without reason and purpose and that we are all connected to the Spirit and each other through the Spirit, then, conversely, I must believe this to be true for all other beings. This realization was a painful one and took me a long time to grasp. I must admit I still struggle from time to time with this one, as I endeavor to remove more layers of the I over me. If this was all true for me and everything happening in my life was happening for me, then it must be for Marie as well. How could this be? How could all the pain I was feeling and had felt be serving a purpose for her and me and for us? This is where it all begins in relationships really: the awareness that any relationship—or at least a healthy one—is the joining of two healthy individuals who are light in themselves, on their way to enlightenment, even completely unconscious, or any combination of these.

Relationships can be our best test and path to enlightenment, as they in one form or another define the journey and lost feelings that we all have because of our entanglement in the fabric and our separation from the Spirit. In an unconscious state and with that deep sense of needing something more, we turn to relationships to fill that void, thinking they will save us and provide salvation. It feels like our love for another and his or her love for us provides the feeling of bliss we yearn for and fulfills our inner purpose.

The poisonous dart here is that no one can provide this for us. This love we are searching for comes through us from the Spirit and can be shared but not provided as a soul source for anyone.

This love only comes through our relationship with ourselves and the Great Spirit. All relationships based on the premise that we are getting what we need from another being or form are codependent and are fed like an addiction until at some point our wheels fall off and we are forced to face our realities. We hope we begin the wake up at this point and become enlightened to our true inner purpose.

This addiction is no different than any other, and all the outcomes are predictable. The waves of failed marriages and single parents right now point to only one thing: collectively, our wheels are falling off right now as our souls are screaming for true happiness and enlightenment. I believe that this is an indication of our time and the necessity for us as a human race to find our connection to the Spirit so we can fulfill our inner purpose and save ourselves from certain extinction. The only thing that can save the human race is our enlightenment. We must wake up and through the love provided by the Great Spirit begin serving one another and our Mother Earth for a greater good.

We are coming out of a century in which we as humans have killed over 100 million of each other in the search for happiness. Our egos are so huge that they will not allow us to see through the eyes of our inner beings, and when the questions begin to arise from deep inside, a profound sadness, which we cannot understand, envelopes us and we start looking outward for answers. That is where Marie and I found ourselves not so many months ago. Our different life journeys were culminating in a sadness that raised questions about our current situations and forced us into making severe and extreme choices in an attempt to alleviate the sadness. The truth all along was that the questions causing the sadness were coming from within, and all the answers required to fulfill our inner purpose were only available from the source of the questions.

MARIE

The sadness and questions started for Marie. Where she was at the time was a culmination of many lifetimes added to her current lifetime of lessons and hardships, all leading her to this second in her life. She had suffered sexual abuse from every father figure in her life from childhood to adolescence, emotional abuse by those closest to her all through her childhood and the significant loss of loved ones, including her mom at a very young age. This coupled with the fact that she had been involved with someone for 20 years who, like her, was unhappy to begin with and trying to fill that happiness void with a codependent relationship was a recipe for relationship disaster and a magical recipe for the beginning of a spiritual journey that would free both of our souls. Her journey led her to another man, who provided lessons and opportunities for her to begin to see and understand who she really was. This man was also being provided the same opportunities through the Great Spirit to fulfill his inner purpose, whether or not he has begun the awakening process I am not sure, but forgiveness truly comes through the understanding that he also was exactly where he was supposed to be and worthy of the same love we all are through the Great Spirit. It is impossible for two egos to survive this sort of opportunity or even for one to survive, as I think is evident by the number and rates of divorce and separation. When left unchecked, our egos attack with a relentless need to be right and feel like the victim. It is only through our self-awareness that we begin to realize what the lessons are and where the sadness comes from.

No one is safe from the process. Thanks to the Great Spirit, all of our destinies are the same: to become light and reconnected on a conscious level with our Creator. As for Marie and me, the opportunity is truly a gift, as we have both begun to wake up and find ourselves through this process and are in very similar time lines fulfilling our inner purposes together. We don't look past each second now, although we slip from time to time. We encourage one another through intense presence not to worry about the past or the future and just be truly in the second and act in our integrity with truth and love. It is through our individual journeys to the light that we now can truly begin to appreciate one another for what we are: beautiful, connected, independent energies who need for nothing, as we are both loved through the Great Spirit. Now, rather than depending on each other for true happiness, we are endeavoring to bring true happiness to a relationship and enjoy each second for what it brings. Our hope is that this will affect those around us and provide opportunities for many others to find their way.

It appears that relationships at an unconscious level can only be dysfunctional with each participant trying to fill a void through the connection with the other. This dysfunction should be embraced at this stage as beautiful, as it provides countless life and being lessons that need only be heard or noticed to begin the enlightenment process. It is this dysfunction in many cases that provides the stimulus to enlightenment for whoever is listening.

WALKING THE ROAD TOGETHER
(THE LONG AND WINDING ROAD)

It is these relationships that afford us each the opportunity to see ourselves through our reflections in our partner. When things happen or situations arise, the way we react to them is based purely on our individual level of consciousness and accumulation of life experiences and pain. Our reaction to stimuli belongs to each of us and each of us alone. No one can decide how you are going to react to a particular stimulus, and through the higher levels of consciousness and enlightenment, one's reaction becomes a choice of being, not a choice of ego. As our level of enlightenment increases, the ego's need to participate in life drama and feed on it becomes secondary.

As we truly begin to see our connection and fulfill our inner purpose, the power of the ego is diminished. As this power diminishes, we are able to be our true selves and not get involved or react to the stimulus, just see it for what it is and let it go. If I have learned one lesson about relationships, it would be this: the feelings associated with realizing that you are something more than what your life situation has invented are intense, and if they are not understood, it becomes very easy for each of us to confuse this unhappy feeling with our partner or life situation. That is where we start to search for a solution to our unhappiness, and inevitably, the search begins externally with a lot of the blame being directed at our partner or life circumstances.

The unhappy feelings have little or nothing to do with our current partner or life situation where enlightenment is involved; they come from a yearning deep inside us to wake up and fulfill our inner purpose. It isn't until we look inside and resolve these feelings for what they are that we can truly begin to heal and wake up. Luke made mention while discussing these issues that sometimes we just have to play the hand we are dealt. The options for each of us really are only twofold in any given second: play or fold. When it comes to relationships, with the exception of those involving abuse, until we have looked deep inside to find our true selves and taken steps to heal our outer selves, folding and trying to find another relationship or situation will be cursed. We will find the same issues we have always had, as they are not partner or place issues; they are ours. It is the lessons and opportunities provided through our circumstances and relationships that give us the growth we need to find our inner purpose. As we wake up and realize where the opportunity truly lives, we can direct our efforts inside and just let the external world be.

As we begin to trust in our Creator and this process, we submit or accept each second for exactly what it is. It is through this acceptance that the pain we create by resisting subsides into being. It is through being that we begin to celebrate the *now* and our connection to the source. When we realize this connection and reveal the vast and endless abundance of love that is available to us all, we can begin to share it with another person. Through the realization that no one and nothing can make us happy, we can truly be happy with anyone. By playing our cards, we are given the opportunity to learn as much as possible from the afforded opportunity. The trick is to see the hands for what they are; at any given moment, each of us holds many hands and a vast number of cards, some intertwined and some independent, but all with an intended lesson and opportunity.

Play each hand as best you can, and take heed of the learning and healing even if it comes sometime down the road. Don't rush or force anything, and don't resist the cards. They are what they are; you are still you. It's not the cards that define you; it's how you play them. Folding of hands to avoid pain and suffering will only force you to play them again later, as the lessons and healing are required at some point if not right now. If you do fold hands, don't fuss; the opportunity will arise again and when received, it transforms into a gift. It is the accumulation of these gifts from our Creator that culminate in our transformation into enlightened beings and the fulfilling of our inner purpose. Everything happens exactly as it is supposed to, so no mistakes can be made. There are only opportunities for gifts to be created. When we are ready to receive it, the gift will be offered. The choice to accept this time or next is ours; all we have to do is shut up and listen.

Shut up and listen. It seems easy enough, but in fact, it is not something that any of us are any good at when we first try. To listen to the Spirit's and the universe's messages, it is paramount that we shut up and listen. We need to quiet our heads and listen with our senses and our hearts. A lifetime of thinking and always being in our heads makes it seem impossible, but we must shut off our minds to hear the messages. Meditation is a great life tool to allow us to practice the art of mindlessness. Meditation is, in essence, the practice of being where we learn to use our heads as a tool only when required and then return to just being. While practicing meditation, we can catch ourselves drifting into our minds, and with gentle correction, we can return to mindless meditation and all that it offers. When meditating, we experience that blissful feeling of this second and the ease of not letting our incessant thoughts rule our lives. Through meditation, we can concentrate on shutting off our thoughts and truly enjoying just being. Through this intentional practice, we can begin to live our lives this way and control the mind and the ego. Meditation also allows us to see deep inside and recognize issues. Once these issues are recognized and the healing process initiated, we are offered the opportunity for healing and growth, a true gift from the Creator. Many other experiences can be offered through meditation—from past-life recognition to visions—and all truly are gifts. From my perspective, though, the single most important focus of meditation should be mindless being and the experience of the feeling that offers. That feeling is available to each of us all the time; all we have to do is get out of our heads and just be. Could anything be easier? When we can successfully get out of our heads on a consistent basis and just be, our lives are transformed. We no longer spend energy wondering about, pondering, or inventing our lives, we just live them without all the garbage created by our mind's and ego's control over them.

GREAT SPIRIT

During meditation one evening in a hot bath with many candles and some sweetgrass burning, I began to understand what the Great Spirit is. The terms given it by a wide variety of religions, although well intended, miss the mark and only confuse the issue for those not yet aware of their purpose. Those who are already feel it. Various figures over the centuries have been identified by religions as saviors and sons of God. We are all saviors and sons and daughters of God; these religious figures idealized in the Bible, the Koran and other holy books were just very enlightened people during a time when most were asleep.

An attempt to explain in words what the Great Spirit is, to give it definition, is an effort in futility. The Great Spirit is so vast, so enormous, so interconnected, and yet so simple that words do not exist to explain or define it for anyone. In fact, as soon as one tries to define or explain it, it is broken and lost in human words and individual conditioning, by either the awakened or the sleeping. The Great Spirit is everything and is everywhere; it is an individual and a sum of all its parts, and it is all of the above. I will try to explain what the Great Spirit is to me only in the spirit of this book for the purpose of trying to convey what I have come to know as the truth. Please understand that any words I come up with will fall extremely short of the mark and are only intended to act as a guide for you so you can begin to understand what has become a profound truth for me.

The science is already there and accepted by the masses; we are nothing more than the concentration and accumulation of molecules, protons, neutrons and electrons of different shapes and sizes concentrated into a physical form that because of its makeup vibrates at a specific frequency. The higher the frequency at which our forms vibrate, the closer to the frequency of the Great Spirit and the universe we become. It is when we can very closely match the frequency of the universe that we begin to mesh with and connect to the Great Spirit. Everything we experience is energy and is given life by the Great Spirit, which, in essence, is the total accumulation of the energy that it gives and accepts freely. The Great Spirit is us, and we are the Great Spirit. It is in the air we breathe and the water we drink; it is in our dreams and everyday life. We are but a fleck of energy sent forth and given form by the Spirit to experience life on its behalf; it is through this life experience that we get the opportunities every second that provide the growth we require to realize our connection and true purpose. It really is that simple and that complex. It is not hard to see how very enlightened people, like Jesus of Nazareth, through the years could have been seen and held in high acclaim by those who recognized the connection and feared and tortured by those who were fast asleep and driven by ego. These saviors were no different than you or I; they had just become very aware of their true purpose and very connected with the source: the Great Spirit.

For me, the understanding I have been gifted with explains religious questions I have had for this entire lifetime, regarding the similarities and huge hypocrisies in all religions. The toughest for me to reconcile over the years was that God was all forgiving but if you broke a rule, you were going to hell—that God was a large, robed, bearded man, who sat in judgment of us all and ruled as a religious leader based on a very specific rule book; all mistakes were handled punitively. That is why I can't use the word *God* anymore; the attempts to define and reconcile the concept for ourselves and one another over the centuries has left us all terribly confused about this word, and as a collective mass, we still search for our answers externally. Our salvation individually and collectively will come when we stop looking outward for our answers and just quietly connect once again to the Great Spirit, our source and Creator. When we get back there, to our common inner purpose, we can and will begin to heal ourselves and our planet. It will be when each little fleck of energy has become aware through the opportunities provided by the Spirit over however many lifetimes are required to get there that we will be welcomed back into the Great Spirit collectively and be one with our Creator. When all of us, every soul, have reached that frequency and have been welcomed home, the Spirit will be whole again and everything in our universe will vibrate as one. We will experience the place called heaven, and it won't matter anymore where or what it is because we will have found it from within and it will just be.

ENGAGEMENT

After much conversation, walking, soul-searching, meditation and consultation and six months after Marie moved out, here we were discussing the possibility of her moving back in. For both of us, the awakening has been swift and the learning curve steep. Both of us are working hard to remain present and accept our seconds as they are; both of us slip from time to time into the past or future; both of us are much more patient with each other since we recognize our egos. We no longer wear our wedding rings, which adorned our fingers for such a long time. I have often been asked why, and my response is always the same: "Not sure." The relationship still has four involved, the I inside of me times two, but for us now, with the gift of conscious love, it's the I's that are present the majority of the time, and the me's, although they will always be there, are not allowed to steer as often.

As we experience our new selves, the pressure is always there to compare what was or what might be and even to bring up the past, which we have affectionately named our elephant in the room. It has become clear to me that expectations of the relationship—or anything else for that matter—are the poison to the present and once placed, immediately push or pull you away from the only thing that can possibly matter. That doesn't mean it doesn't happen; it just means that when it does, it is the return to consciousness through awareness and presence that allows us to get back to enjoying those seconds.

These pressures don't always come from within. Often, they are provided by friends, family, or even strangers or situations. The pressure allows for contrast and growth, and although it is difficult to navigate through at times, it is always a gift. A short while after we agreed to live together again and experience our new moments together, our oldest son proposed to his girlfriend. The act was preceded by many questions: "Dad, is the ring big enough? Dad, how much should the wedding cost? Dad, should I ask her dad first? Dad, is this the right thing to do?" Wow! This was huge for me. I had no idea how much programming I was dealing with and had to consider my answers and actions carefully to ensure I didn't push anything on these kids that was not from my heart. It took some time and much respect for Jake and Cat and their places in the fabric to formulate a response to the questions and the situation. These kids were exactly where they were supposed to be, the timing divine and their journeys well underway. The last thing I wanted to do was push anything that might be life programming or collective unconsciousness into their world. At the same time, I needed to respect the journeys of everyone in their circle without putting a blanket over my own. All I could do was share my experience and feelings and ask that they do what made their souls smile. I advised them to pray for the Great Spirit to guide them on their path.

"Jake," I said, "you remember when you were a kid and we talked about religion and I told you to listen to all the information available and to your heart to figure out how you felt about it? That is how you need to approach marriage and life. Use your brain to sort the information, and let your heart guide you through your soul's connection to the Spirit.

"When I got married many years ago, it was because that was how it worked: you got a job, found a girl, got married, bought a house and started having kids. Your mom and I operated from the confused subconscious, and not knowing what we didn't know, proceeded to execute all of the programs placed in our ponds over the past years of this lifetime and others. One of the toughest for me to reconcile was the religious aspect, having been raised Roman Catholic; the programming around marriage and divorce was very clear, as it is among most religions. But why is that? How can anyone guarantee anything through vows or any other means other than to do their very best in each second and share the love provided by our Creator? To love each other during sickness or in health until death do us part? I am sorry, Son, but *no*. That expectation is unfair and unrealistic. It only adds extreme amounts of pressure to a couple of kids who need only commit to one thing—each other—for every second afforded by the Spirit. If you can commit, through vows or whatever form you feel works, to sharing divine love with this person every second and through whatever future seconds hold, you will love also. That is really all that you can commit to." It was at that second in my life that I realized why I no longer wore my wedding ring. It was another experience offered by the Spirit for the opportunity to grow just a little closer to it through the connection of paths and interaction in the seconds.

As divorce rates climb and people become increasingly unsure or confused, I see a clear indication of vast awakenings. It is not to be feared but endeared, as our souls gain the space required to allow us to be aware that we are not only this suit of skin, but at the core of our being, a perfect soul with a purpose. We are all on our journeys and exactly where we are supposed to be. We are connected to it all. As we begin to awaken and deal with our new awareness, we start to externalize the feelings and the reasons we are having them. This brings an automatic ego response: someone or something else is causing this discomfort, and if I can only fix them or get it, I will be happy. The truth is all the answers are within, and it is through this process that we begin to search for those answers. As we are all on this journey and in beautifully different spots and lifetimes, reconciling our individual awareness and receiving our aha moments or epiphanies, as Marie calls them, we find ourselves in many cases surrounded by people who have not heard their names called yet. These people can be friends and coworkers, family, even strangers, or, as is the case in over 50 percent of marriages, spouses.

As we are awakened, the I inside of the me becomes aware that it is there and that it has a purpose. The work then begins to give it more space to feel and be. In many cases, marriages begin with the me's driving with very little awareness of the I's inside. Through subconscious programs and ego, they begin their lives together—as that is understood by their individual subconscious programs. In our case, we ran these programs for 20 years not knowing what we didn't know. Then, for us, an event called Marie's name, and the awareness arose for her that there was something inside. The discomfort made her go looking for what that might be exactly as intended. As she began to shift from me to I, I was still stuck in me and our problems began. It is exceedingly difficult to be in the presence of a being who is sound asleep when you have begun to awaken, and as you progress toward the light, the darkness of being asleep can seem an impossible challenge. This is why many gurus and enlightened beings tell us to surround ourselves at least some of the time with people who are in similar places on their journeys. It allows us to be where we are with understanding, compassion and love—and without judgment. As that separation grows from light to dark, it can become impossible to remain together and as was intended from the beginning. It may become necessary to continue on these journeys separately. Recognition of these differences and the ability to give each other the space to journey, whether it be together or apart, brings great peace. As seems to be the case in a majority of marriages today, people are awakening at different times with different events, and this is causing much dis-ease in married couples. Many times, one partner begins to awaken while the other is still fast asleep, and this may not change in this lifetime. In our case, Marie's journey provided my wake-up

JAMES GRACE

call and the awareness of the I inside of me. As we began to search for balance and peace internally, we realized that our paths were coming together again and we could journey together. The difference for us both was the awareness that our individual peace and happiness had to come from within and in order to be happy as a couple, we first had to be happy as individuals. I believe this is where the phrase "I love you" originated. The meaning for me now is "Love you, and when you can love you and I can love me, there will be boundless amounts of that love to share." Love you, Marie.

The awareness does not mean immediate bliss and happiness, although at times, that buzz of presence and awareness is intoxicating and highly addictive. To the contrary, our journeys sometimes seem very dark and difficult with hours and days spent in the sandbox. A very dear friend of mine explained to me one day that these dark days were necessary, as it is with the contrast that we can find the light. As one cup of light is poured into our souls, an equal amount of darkness must be poured out and that can be very painful for the me. "The soul would have no rainbow if the eyes had no tears." Each ebb and flow from dark to light heightens the balance of light and increases our love for self and the amount available to be shared. When we are gifted with a life partner to grow with, the increased amount of love and support available can catapult us to heights that cannot be described and then provide our lifelines out of those dark days. One of my greatest gifts was to find myself travelling once again with Marie, and to have that opportunity in this speck in time is truly divine.

THE END

I have struggled with an ending for this book since I wrote down the first word. Now, here I sit, December 21, 2011, exactly 12 months from the day the Mayan calendar ends. Some say the earth will be consumed by fire, hit by a meteorite, or taken over by robots or aliens. Some say that is the day a critical mass of enlightened humans will be achieved, and a shift in consciousness will happen, much like in *Avatar*. Some say nothing will happen. One thing is for certain, the world is in turmoil—billions are starving, severe weather is becoming more frequent and more violent, and plants and animals are going extinct at unprecedented rates. World monetary systems are collapsing, there are increasing police actions by our governments, people are screaming for sense, marriages are failing, and kids are lost while being labelled the "useless generation." Indigenous peoples are waking up and demanding acknowledgement and retribution. There is just a general feeling that things are not right anymore.

The ending for this story, my marriage, my kids and my humanity has not been written. Even though there is obviously some interest in the ending, my focus is going to be on each second of my journey with an absolute trust that through love and appreciation for each moment, the ending will be exactly as it is supposed to be. I accept that our journey is our gift and memories of past moments and expectations of future outcomes are simply making us miss the only thing that really is—right now. The truth is the memories and the ending will only be good if we can live the present awake, enlightened and with love.

I spend my moments where they are, and the good ones and bad ones bring peace and love. When I have ego moments, I work to get back to the I inside of me and forgive myself the slip, grateful for the opportunity to grow and learn. I see all of humanity as equal and connected and send love and light every chance I get. I recognize that we are all at different points in the fabric and work hard to meet humanity where they are with love and compassion. I trust that we will end up exactly where we are meant to and that the only way is through love . . . Love is all we need.

Science and spirituality have converged again, each complementing the other. It makes sense to feel those feelings and walk the red path, enjoying every step and completing your purpose. Wake up, and become enlightened about who you truly are. It really is that simple. Our individual purposes really are that important; you really are that important. Just like our bodies are constructed of billions of single cells, our humanity is constructed of billions of individuals and our universe of billions of planetary bodies all connected, all one, all grandfather. Peace, love and light to all my brothers and sisters, the winged, the four-legged and the two-legged—all the standing people and their relations. A great man has said that the physical form is just an instrument of the soul; it will be when we realize this and begin to use it this way with love that there will once again be heaven on earth.